TRUEBLOOD™

TRUE BLOOD

Eats, Drinks, and Bites
from Bon Temps

Gianna Sobol and Alan Ball
WITH Karen Sommer Shalett

RECIPES BY Marcelle Bienvenu

FOOD PHOTOGRAPHS BY Alex Farnum

CHRONICLE BOOKS
SAN FRANCISCO

HBO

www.hbo.com

Library of Congress Cataloging-in-Publication
Data:

Ball, Alan, 1957–

True blood : eats, drinks, and bites from
Bon Temps / by Gianna Sobol and Alan
Ball; with Karen Sommer Shalett and
Marcelle Bienvenu.

pages cm

ISBN 978-1-4521-1086-8

1. Cooking, American—Louisiana style.
2. True blood (Television program)
I. Shalett, Karen Sommer. II. Bienvenu,
Marcelle. III. Title.

TX715.2.L68B357 2012
641.59763—dc23
2011048550

Manufactured in China
Design by Public
Prop styling by Christine Wolheim
Food styling by Lillian Kang

True Blood series photographs by Prashant Gupta,
Doug Hyun, John P. Johnson, and Jamie Trueblood.
Special thanks to James Costos, Stacey Abiraj,
Josh Goodstadt, Janis Fein, Cara Grabowski,
Robin Eisgrau, Ron Vecchiarelli, Marlis Pujol,
Tom Bozzelli, Amanda Poulsen, Dawn Yanagihara,
Deborah Kops, Ellen Wheat, and Ken Della Penta.

10 9 8 7 6 5 4 3 2 1

Chronicle Books LLC
680 Second Street
San Francisco, CA 94107
www.chroniclebooks.com

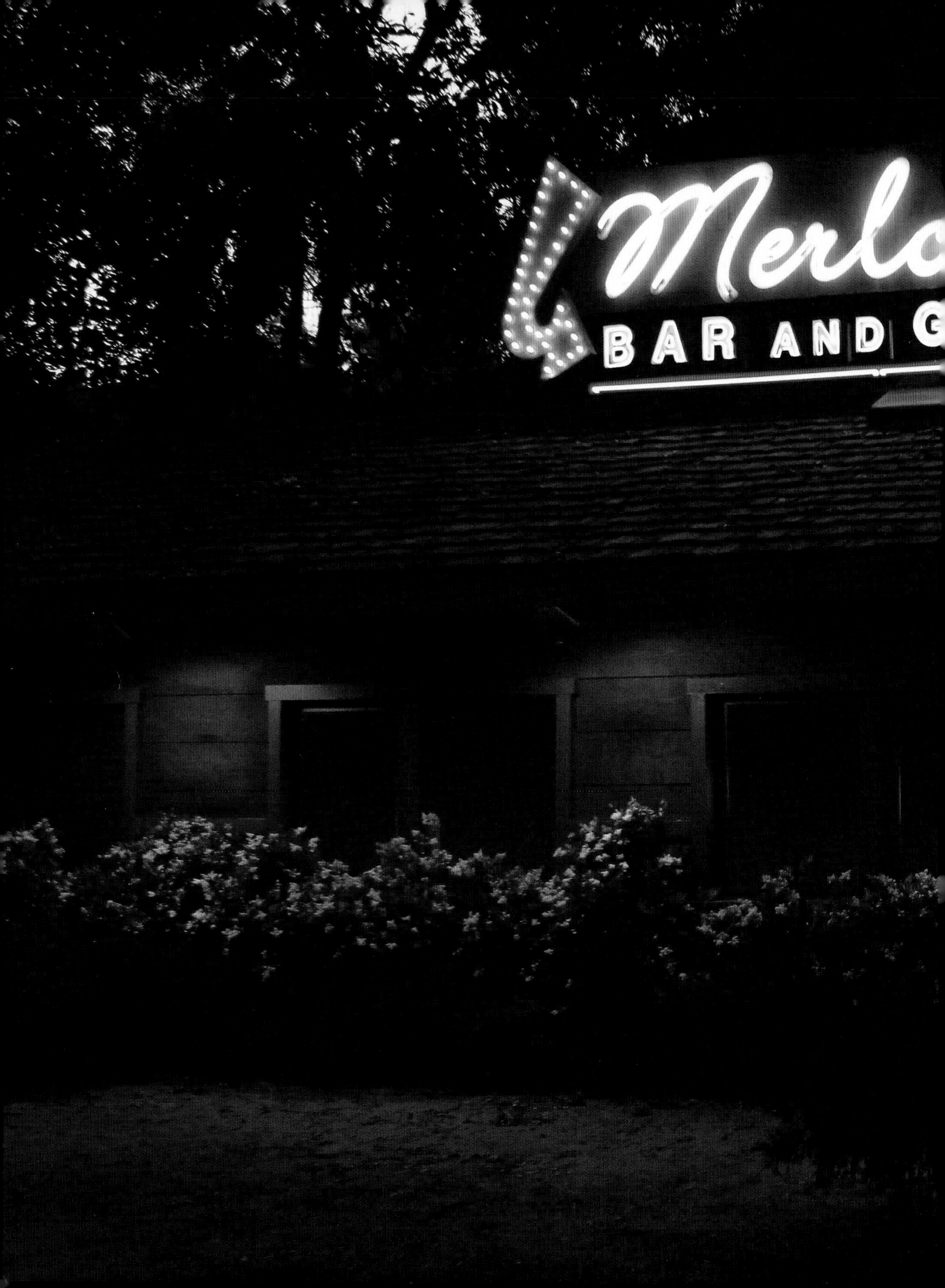
Merlo
BAR AND G

DRINKS TO DIE FOR

LOU PINE'S BIKER BAR
By Alcide Herveaux

HOME COOKIN'

Fangtasia

EATING OUT IN BON TEMPS

Preface

I grew up in a small town in the South, so fried chicken, grits, and succotash were a part of my everyday life. My mother's green bean casserole, forever seared into my taste buds' memory, holds a very dear place in my heart. So when I sat down to write a show about the people of Bon Temps, Louisiana, it was no wonder that so much of their lives would revolve around food. It feels tremendously organic for the drama (and comedy) to go down over pitchers of Abita and burgers at Merlotte's, or blood cocktails over at Fangtasia, or while chowing down on leftover pie at Gran's. So read, cook, and, by god, taste Summer's biscuits. We've invited you into our kitchens, and now you can take us into yours.

—Alan Ball

Introduction

BY SOOKIE STACKHOUSE

I always thought I was lucky to be born in Bon Temps. Sure, there's a lotta drama for such a small town, but the people here are really somethin' special. And as different as we may be from each other, we've all got one thing in common: we love good food. So whether you're joinin' us for supper at Merlotte's, or even just openin' a lunch pail at Jason's road-crew site, you're enjoyin' somebody's cookin'. It's one of the best ways we can show just how much we care. I don't know if it's a Bon Temps thing, a Louisiana thing, or just a people thing, but I know it's true here.

I've heard about all those fancy restaurants in Chicago and New York, servin' crawfish étouffée, with a white tablecloth 'n' all. But between you an' me, the best of it can be found here in Renard Parish in Lafayette's kitchen. Whether you wanna call it Cajun, Low-Country, Bayou, or even just good ole fashioned Southern cookin', when it's done right, it doesn't matter if you dress it up with fancy linen. No étouffée from the big city can compete. It takes real Louisianans to teach you how to turn grease into gravy.

So we decided to do just that by puttin' together this cookbook. We've got Gran's fried chicken and her sugar pie, Terry's chili, crazy Maryann's maenad feast, Tara's and my ice cream sundae parties, and all the rest of the recipes that we grew up on. And for those who prefer their food in liquid form, like our vampire friends, we've got a whole section on mixin' up cocktails.

Just the other night, I showed Bill and Jessica a few of the recipes. I was real excited and wanted to hear what they had to say about it, but they both got real quiet. I think it was because they couldn't eat any of the dishes I was showin' 'em. Jessica started cryin' blood tears, and then Bill finally spoke up and said he would be spendin' the rest of the night thinkin' about his family and what they'd eaten together.

That's the point, I suppose. Food memories are some of the best we got. Sittin' down to eat with the people you love, or even just like, life don't get much better than that. Least not here in Bon Temps.

Drinks to Die For

COCKTAILING, FANGTASIA STYLE

BY ERIC NORTHMAN

The idea of coming out of the coffin, or mainstreaming, as the American Vampire League puts it, never made any sense to me. For thousands of years, vampires had a pretty good thing going. But the Authority makes the rules, and when they went through with the so-called Great Revelation, I just shook my head and figured out the best way to benefit from it. Now, we'd heard of underground places where humans and vampires would associate with one another. Before we came out of the coffin, those places were understandably dangerous to humans (and less understandably, humans would still seek them out). But in a world of vampire-human coexistence, why not give the people what they want: a legitimate venue for humans to indulge their curiosity and vampires to indulge their appetites. With Pam's unique taste in decor, we quickly arrived at a motif: Southern Vampire Gothic, which meant ordering some things from Romania and others from Walmart.

Since the night we opened our doors, Fangtasia has been very lucrative, and we've even inspired other vampire bars across the country. Besides the money, there are plenty of other benefits to Fangtasia. I do have my little romper room in the basement, where I can interview my pick of any new talent. And it's the perfect place to host a whole slew of questionable activities. Like selling V for Sophie-Anne or temporarily storing humans like Lafayette Reynolds. The police and other human authorities are afraid to come here, and I am the vampire sheriff of Area 5, so opposition is pretty minimal.

The only downside to owning a bar is running the place. That means the usual business minutiae: matching receipts, making sure that busboys get paid out, keeping things legit enough to ensure that the IRS and local tax boards are happy, and most important, finding good help. The only vampire a vampire can trust is the one he made, so I brought Pam along with me every step of the way. Sure we had the Longshadow incident, but just like any other mishaps in my life, the situation got corrected. Mostly I just like seeing the humans' alleged moral high ground crumble in the face of all that is vampire. We're better looking. We're more sophisticated. We're more fun. That's what humans come here to find out. I'm always happy to serve them. And I don't mean for dinner.

Ruby Mixer

MAKES 6 OUNCES

BY NAN FLANAGAN

When Louis Pasteur (yes, he's a vampire) and the Japanese got together in the 1980s, there was no stopping them. They created Tru Blood, a synthetic blood substitute, allowing vampires to come out of the coffin. But fangbangers and friends have long wanted to taste what their vampire pals drink at bars like Fangtasia, so some enterprising mortals created a version for humans that goes by the same name. You can order Tru Blood at www.trubeverage.com or use this recipe to concoct a similar drink. Keep in mind, there's only one original. But sometimes you just need a quick fix. The synthetic blood substitute's substitute.

4 OUNCES	CARBONATED ORANGE SODA, SUCH AS ORANGINA OR SAN PELLEGRINO ARANCIATA
1½ OUNCES	GRENADINE
ABOUT 1 TABLESPOON	FRESH LEMON JUICE

Combine the orange soda, grenadine, and lemon juice
in a pitcher. Stir to blend before using.

Dead on the Beach

BY LONGSHADOW

There are plenty of sorority girls—or live bait as I like to call them—who come to Fangtasia looking for adventure. I'd like to be dead on a beach with a few of them, but until closing time I'm stuck behind the bar serving up my special cocktail. Nothing like a little vodka to loosen them up just enough for a predawn taste.

1½ OUNCES	VODKA
½ OUNCE	PEACH SCHNAPPS
3 OUNCES	TRU BLOOD OR RUBY MIXER (PAGE 23)
1 OUNCE	FRESH ORANGE JUICE
CRACKED ICE	
ORANGE TWIST	FOR GARNISH

Combine the vodka, schnapps, Tru Blood, and orange juice in a cocktail shaker. Shake or stir. Fill a highball glass with ice and pour the mixture over the ice. Garnish with the orange twist. Serve immediately.

MAKES 1 DRINK

Tequila Moonrise

BY DEBBIE PELT

Gettin' off V was the hardest thing I've ever done, but it was worth it for Alcide. Now I ain't supposed to be drinkin', bein' a recoverin' addict, but sometimes I just have to take the edge off. When I get to thinkin' about how Alcide runs to Sookie's rescue every time she gets herself into some kind of sh*t, I mix myself a special treat. Don't tell Alcide, or he'll be madder than a wet hen.

1 ½ OUNCES	TEQUILA
CRACKED ICE	
1 ½ OUNCES	TRU BLOOD OR RUBY MIXER (PAGE 23)
¾ OUNCE.........................	GRENADINE
ORANGE SLICE	FOR GARNISH
MARASCHINO CHERRY	FOR GARNISH

Pour the tequila into a highball glass filled with ice and top with the Tru Blood. Tilt the glass and add the grenadine by pouring it down the side of the glass and then flipping the bottle vertically very quickly. The grenadine should go straight to the bottom of the glass and rise slowly through the drink. Garnish with the orange slice and cherry. Serve immediately.

The Necromancer

BY MARNIE STONEBROOK

It's hard not to need a little liquid courage when all your life you've been made to feel so scared of your own shadow. I'd been afraid too long, so I made a pomegranate potion to get the confidence I needed to raise Minerva from the dead. I drank it again before I prayed for Antonia to come to me. And after our communion, I didn't have much need for this kind of spirit. I had the real thing.

CRACKED ICE

3½ OUNCES ....TRU BLOOD OR RUBY MIXER (PAGE 23)

1 OUNCE ....CHERRY-FLAVORED RUM

½ OUNCE..........................POMEGRANATE LIQUEUR

MARASCHINO CHERRY ......FOR GARNISH

MAKES 1 DRINK

Fill a lowball (or old-fashioned) glass with ice. Pour the Tru Blood, rum, and pomegranate liqueur over the ice. Stir and garnish with the cherry. Serve immediately.

Lovin' in the Coven

BY LAFAYETTE REYNOLDS

There's always been this darkness in my crazy, f***ed-up family. So when Jesus showed me his magic, it gave me the motherf***in' heebie-jeebies. Jesus has got on his demon face and some bitch is divin' down my throat, and he's still tryin' to convince me this freakiness is some sorta gift? That cute bitch's head ain't on right. Bein' a medium is f***ed the f***ed up, and sometimes this hooker needs a drink just to get through the day. Cheers, bitches.

2 OUNCES	CITRUS VODKA
1 OUNCE	FRESH LEMON JUICE
½ OUNCE	SIMPLE SYRUP (FACING PAGE)
DASH	EGG WHITE
CRACKED ICE	
½ OUNCE	TRU BLOOD OR RUBY MIXER (PAGE 23)
LEMON TWIST	FOR GARNISH

Combine the vodka, lemon juice, simple syrup, and egg white in a cocktail shaker filled with ice. Shake and strain into a chilled lowball (or old-fashioned) glass. Float the Tru Blood on the surface of the drink and garnish with the lemon twist. Serve immediately.

Simple Syrup

½ CUP	SUGAR
4 OUNCES	WATER

Combine the sugar and water in a small saucepan over medium-high heat and bring to a boil. Reduce the heat to medium-low and simmer, stirring to dissolve the sugar completely, 6 to 8 minutes. Remove from the heat and let cool completely. Transfer the syrup to an airtight container and refrigerate for at least 1 hour before using. The syrup will keep in the refrigerator for up to 2 weeks.

MAKES 8 OUNCES

The William T. Compton

BY WILLIAM THOMAS COMPTON

When I was first lieutenant in the Twenty-eighth Louisiana Infantry, Toliver Humphries and I would drink ginger beer and talk for hours, until I quieted the memory of the family I'd left back home in Bon Temps. I can no longer imbibe as I used to, but I've recently begun mixing this libation for humans who join me for a drink. It covers the metallic taste of Tru Blood, and watching them enjoy it gives me a nostalgia that makes me feel almost . . . human.

MAKES 1 DRINK

1 ½ OUNCES	ORANGE VODKA
½ OUNCE	FRESH LIME JUICE
3 OUNCES	GINGER BEER
3 OUNCES	TRU BLOOD OR RUBY MIXER (PAGE 23)
CRACKED ICE	
ORANGE WEDGE	FOR GARNISH

Pour the vodka, lime juice, ginger beer, and Tru Blood into a highball glass filled with ice. Garnish with the orange wedge. Serve immediately.

Blood and Sand

BY LORENA KRASIKI

MAKES 1 DRINK

Forget Capone. The carnage William Compton and I left behind during Prohibition made even the St. Valentine's Day Massacre look like a paltry bar fight. It may not be evident now, but there was a time when my progeny was just as sadistic as me. I can't smell cherry brandy without thinking of those high times before I released Bill. Life— or death, really—just hasn't been the same since.

1½ OUNCES	....	SCOTCH WHISKY
1½ OUNCES	....	CHERRY BRANDY
1½ OUNCES	....	SWEET VERMOUTH
1½ OUNCES	....	FRESH ORANGE JUICE
CRACKED ICE		
ORANGE TWIST	....	FOR GARNISH

Pour the Scotch, brandy, vermouth, and orange juice into a cocktail shaker filled with ice. Shake well and strain into a cocktail glass. Garnish with the orange twist. Serve immediately.

Dead or Alive

BY JESUS VELASQUEZ

MAKES 1 DRINK

I told Lafayette I was a brujo, and I brought him to meet my abuelo because I knew there was magic in him so powerful, only a man like Don Bartolo could convince him of its truth. So how much tequila would you drink after finding out you're a medium? Lafayette downed three canteens full of this stuff on the drive back to Bon Temps. He told me, "Honey, the bite on this cocktail is about as strong as that motherf***in' rattlesnake."

2 OUNCES	TEQUILA
4 OUNCES	TOMATO JUICE
½ TEASPOON	PREPARED HORSERADISH
3 DASHES	TABASCO SAUCE
½ TEASPOON	PICKLED JALAPEÑO JUICE
SQUEEZE	FRESH LIME JUICE
SALT	
CRACKED ICE	
PICKLED JALAPEÑO	FOR GARNISH

Combine the tequila, tomato juice, horseradish, Tabasco, and jalapeño juice in a cocktail shaker. Add the lime juice and season with salt. Stir. Fill a highball glass with ice and pour the cocktail over the ice. Garnish with the pickled jalapeño. Serve immediately.

Gin and Tonic

BY SOOKIE STACKHOUSE

*When I asked Bill to take me to Fang-
tasia, I knew there'd be vampires and
fangbangers, I just didn't expect to see
all that* leather. *Bill wasn't thrilled
that I wore my best sundress, but I
didn't care. I knew I looked good and
he was runnin' around tellin' everybody
I was* his. *Now, I don't drink much
since it makes it hard to keep the voices
out. But a gin and tonic is pretty much
a gin and tonic no matter where you
drink it, so it seemed like the only safe
thing in there. Other than Bill, of course.*

MAKES 1 DRINK

CRACKED ICE
3 OUNCES.........................GIN
TONIC WATER
1 TEASPOON...................FRESH LIME JUICE
LIME WEDGE...................FOR GARNISH

Fill a highball glass with ice. Add the gin and
enough tonic water to fill the glass. Float the
lime juice on top and garnish with the lime
wedge. Serve immediately.

Mama's Whiskey Sour

BY TARA THORNTON

I been mixin' whiskey sours for my mama since the first grade, and as messed up as that is, it's made me a hell of a bartender at Merlotte's. Sam says I make the best whiskey drinks this side of the Mississippi, and I've got a job there as long as I don't go off on anybody no more. Which I don't, unless they're stupid.

1 ½ OUNCES	BOURBON
4 OUNCES	SWEET AND SOUR MIX (FACING PAGE)
CRACKED ICE	
ORANGE SLICE	FOR GARNISH
MARASCHINO CHERRY	FOR GARNISH

Pour the bourbon and sweet and sour mix into a large lowball (or old-fashioned) glass filled with ice. Stir and garnish with the orange slice and cherry. Serve immediately.

MAKES 1 DRINK

Sweet and Sour Mix

MAKES 3 CUPS

2 CUPS ....FRESH LEMON JUICE
(ABOUT 10 LEMONS)

1 CUP ....SIMPLE SYRUP
(PAGE 33)

Combine the lemon juice and simple
syrup in a glass jar. Stir to blend.
Store in an airtight container in the
refrigerator for up to 1 month.

Bon Temps Bloody Mary

BY ARLENE FOWLER BELLEFLEUR

I know Jessica was made a vampire against her will 'n' all, but I don't feel one bit sorry for her. You know why? She's a goddamned tip hoarder. People love tippin' redheads, and I used to be the only redhead at Merlotte's. Now with that girl battin' her stupid eyelashes at every male customer that walks in the door, I can't get no one to sit in my section! So when my tables are real slow, or just plain empty, I make myself a Bloody Mary and sip it while I watch Mikey play with that stupid doll. It helps pass the time 'til my shift is done and I can get on home to Coby and Lisa.

6 OUNCES	**TOMATO JUICE**
1 ½ OUNCES	**VODKA**
1 TEASPOON	**FRESH LIME JUICE**
½ TEASPOON	**WORCESTERSHIRE SAUCE**
SALT	
FRESHLY GROUND BLACK PEPPER	
CAYENNE PEPPER	
CRACKED ICE	
PICKLED GREEN BEANS OR PICKLED OKRA	**FOR GARNISH**

Combine the tomato juice, vodka, lime juice, and Worcestershire in a cocktail shaker. Season with salt, black pepper, and cayenne. Stir. Fill a highball glass with ice and pour the drink over the ice. Garnish with the beans or okra. Serve immediately.

MAKES 1 DRINK

Reviver

BY HOLLY CLEARY

Being a Wiccan gives you a special sort of insight into the world. That doesn't always mean it's a cakewalk. Just like the material world, the magical world can be unpredictable and scary. Like when Marnie raised her bird from the dead, I was plenty shaken. I made a little somethin' to calm my nerves down before going back home to my boys, Wade and Rocky.

1 ½ OUNCES	GIN
1 ½ OUNCES	COINTREAU
1 ½ OUNCES	LILLET BLANC
1 ½ OUNCES	FRESH LEMON JUICE
DASH	PERNOD
CRACKED ICE	
MARASCHINO CHERRY	FOR GARNISH

Combine the gin, Cointreau, Lillet Blanc, lemon juice, and Pernod in a cocktail shaker filled with ice. Shake well and strain into a lowball (or old-fashioned) glass. Garnish with the cherry. Serve immediately.

Vampade

BY PAM SWYNFORD DE BEAUFORT

I love being a vampire. I have a world of pleasure available to me that humans can only dream of, although there are a few downsides. What makes me ache for my human days? Booze. If only I could still drink to forget a problem— like the irritating blonde who turned my maker into an infatuated tween. Eric going so far as to offer his life for hers? That's the sort of thing that makes me want a dozen Harvey Wallbangers and a stranger to stumble home with. Instead I'll wait for some pouty little thing to get filled up with Vampade and then I'll help myself.

3 OUNCES	TRU BLOOD OR RUBY MIXER (PAGE 23)
CRACKED ICE	
1½ OUNCES	LEMONADE OR SWEET AND SOUR MIX (PAGE 45)
1 OUNCE	BLACKBERRY LIQUEUR
LEMON WEDGE	FOR GARNISH

Pour the Tru Blood into a highball glass filled with ice. Add the lemonade and blackberry liqueur and stir. Garnish with the lemon wedge. Serve immediately.

MAKES 1 DRINK

Blood Royale

BY TALBOT

When my dear Russell came to me centuries ago, he was rather rough around the edges. Of course, I was a royal long before I was made vampire by the future King of Mississippi. I gave him refinement, he gave me eternity. I carried on the sybaritic lifestyle of a Greek prince, creating our own castle and surrounding us with the finest decor, food, and drink. Take this cocktail of chilled, carbonated blood—cruelty-free as the source was a willing donor. Taste that citrus finish? The source ate only tangerines for three days.

CRACKED ICE

1½ OUNCES	SPARKLING WINE, SUCH AS PROSECCO
1½ OUNCES	SWEET VERMOUTH
1½ OUNCES	CAMPARI
SPLASH	TRU BLOOD OR RUBY MIXER (PAGE 23)
SQUEEZE	FRESH LIME JUICE

Put a few pieces of ice in a champagne flute. Pour the sparkling wine, sweet vermouth, and Campari over the ice. Add the splash of Tru Blood and the squeeze of lime juice. Serve immediately.

MAKES 1 DRINK

Gran's Lemonade

BY ADELE STACKHOUSE

The trick to my lemonade is that there's enough sugar to remind you there's always somethin' sweet 'round the corner, even when the sourest of times are comin' on. Sookie needed a lot of that kind of remindin' when she was growin' up. Jason seemed to have the sweet side of life down pat. What he needed was some ice dumped over his head.

2 CUPS	SUGAR
1 ½ CUPS.........................	HOT TAP WATER
1 CUP	FRESH LEMON JUICE
CRACKED ICE	
LEMON SLICES	FOR GARNISH
MINT SPRIGS	FOR GARNISH

Combine the sugar and water in a glass pitcher and stir to dissolve the sugar. Add the lemon juice and stir to blend. Cover and refrigerate until ready to serve.

Fill tall glasses with ice and pour the lemonade over it. Garnish with lemon slices and mint. Serve immediately.

CONTINUED

Killer Lemonade

Purée some fresh or frozen strawberries or raspberries in a blender, and add 1 tablespoon of purée to each glass of lemonade. Stir to mix. Serve immediately.

Sweet Tea

MAKES ABOUT 4 CUPS, 4 TO 6 SERVINGS

BY JASON STACKHOUSE

Why would you drink that store-bought stuff, even in those fancy bottles, when you could have Gran's iced tea? No matter when I'd stop by, Gran would have a jug in the fridge. It didn't much matter what we were eatin'— boudin or chicken-fried steak—I always looked forward to a glass of that sweet tea. Sookie doesn't cook much when I come 'round, and she certainly ain't been makin' tea like Gran used to, so usually I'll just settle for a beer. But when it gets real hot and I'm comin' off a tough road-crew shift? That's when I miss it most.

3 TO 5	TEA BAGS, DEPENDING ON HOW STRONG YOU WANT YOUR TEA
4 CUPS	BOILING WATER
1 CUP	SUGAR
CRACKED ICE	
LEMON WEDGES	FOR GARNISH

Put the tea bags in a heatproof container and pour in the boiling water. Steep for 3 to 5 minutes. Discard the tea bags. Add the sugar while the tea is still warm and stir to dissolve the sugar. Cover and refrigerate for at least 1 hour.

Fill tall glasses with ice and pour in the tea. Garnish with lemon wedges. Serve immediately.

Red Sweet Tea

2 CUPS	BOILING WATER
4	CELESTIAL SEASONINGS RED ZINGER TEA BAGS
1 CUP	SUGAR
CRACKED ICE	

Pour the boiling water over the tea bags in a heatproof container. Steep for 4 to 6 minutes, then discard the tea bags. Add the sugar while the tea is still warm and stir to dissolve the sugar. Add 2 cups cold water, cover, and refrigerate for at least 1 hour.

Fill tall glasses with ice and pour the tea over it. Serve immediately.

MAKES ABOUT 4 CUPS, 4 TO 6 SERVINGS

Light of Day Punch

BY STEVE NEWLIN

When I was human and the founder and face of the Fellowship of the Sun, we aimed to take back the color red from our vampire foes. We used to serve this punch at all our Soldiers of the Sun inductions and toast to our humanity and God's grace. I can't drink it anymore, now that I'm a vampire and all, but I sure do miss the taste. I used to crave it on hot summer days because it was so refreshing. Now? I'm still figuring out just what the heck I'm craving.

2 CUPS	BOILING WATER
6	TEA BAGS
½ CUP	SUGAR
1 CUP	FRESH LEMON JUICE (ABOUT 5 LEMONS)
1 CUP	CRANBERRY JUICE
2 OUNCES	GRENADINE
4 CUPS	COLD GINGER ALE
FRESH MINT SPRIGS	FOR GARNISH

In a large heatproof pitcher or jug, pour the boiling water over the tea bags and let steep for 5 minutes. Discard the bags. Add the sugar to the tea and stir to dissolve. Add the fruit juices and grenadine. Refrigerate for several hours. When ready to serve, add the cold ginger ale. Garnish with mint sprigs. Serve immediately.

MAKES ABOUT 8 CUPS, 8 TO 12 SERVINGS

LOU PINE'S BIKER BAR

BY ALCIDE HERVEAUX

It may not look like much from the outside, but Lou Pine's is the oldest werewolf bar in the state of Mississippi. I'd been tryin' to stay away, what with Cooter and his wolves drinkin' enough for all of us, but Sookie convinced me to walk through those doors again. Sure enough, the scent of that place took me back to the good ole days, when the Jackson pack was what it used to be, and Debbie wasn't hooked on V yet. We'd start the night with a shot of moonshine in our beers, then chase it with a Silver Stake—a whisky and gin mix that leaves you howlin' for more. And we'd always end the evenin' with a Hair of the Wolf, a cocktail from some Cajun friends of the pack.

Silver Stake

CRACKED ICE
½ OUNCE..........................SCOTCH WHISKY
2 OUNCES........................GIN
LEMON TWIST...................FOR GARNISH

Fill a mixing glass with ice and pour the Scotch over the ice. Stir to coat the ice. Drain off the Scotch and discard. Add the gin to the glass, stir, and strain into a martini glass. Garnish with the lemon twist. Serve immediately.

Moonshine Rising

1 ½ OUNCES	**MOONSHINE (OR BOURBON, VODKA, OR TEQUILA)**
12 OUNCES	**COLD BEER, SUCH AS ABITA PURPLE HAZE OR ABITA TURBODOG**

Pour the moonshine into a shot glass. Throw back the shot and then chase it with the beer. Or, pour the shot into the beer and guzzle down.

MAKES 1 DRINK

Hair of the Wolf

4 OUNCES	GIN
½ OUNCE	FRESH LIME JUICE
3 DASHES	TABASCO SAUCE
CRACKED ICE	
1 SLIVER	PEELED FRESH GINGER

Pour the gin, lime juice, and Tabasco into a
cocktail shaker filled with ice. Shake vigorously.
Strain the mixture into a lowball (or old-
fashioned) glass. Garnish with the ginger.
Serve immediately.

Home Cookin'

DOWN-HOME COOKIN'
IN BON TEMPS

BY SOOKIE STACKHOUSE

There was no better place to run to when I was growin' up than Gran's kitchen table. Didn't matter if it was to celebrate an A+ on a spellin' test with sugar pie, or to wallow in some hot chocolate with those tiny little marshmallows when I was missin' my parents. I wasn't the only one, either. Tara spent more time at that table than on any piece a furniture her mama mighta owned. And Jason. Even though he was busy with football practice and all the girls he was sneakin' around with, he always showed up for supper. Specially when Gran had gone and cooked her fried chicken.

Tara and me grew up at that table, eatin' ice cream sundaes, talkin' about whatever girls talk about—boys, pimples, fittin' in, not fittin' in. See, Jason was a star in Bon Temps, so I couldn't talk to him about what I was goin' through. I was a throwaway—people were either scared of me or barely even knew I existed. But Gran always set me right. I'd be busy shovelin' in eggs, sausages, and biscuits and she'd be busy tellin' me I was special and had all these gifts. She never quite gave it a real name, and she usually referred to my bein' able to hear peoples' thoughts as my "ability." It was over a hearty breakfast that she finally told me Grandpa Earl used to know things, too, real personal things nobody ever told him about. He even used his "ability" to stop my great-uncle Francis from tryin' to kill himself. The first time, anyways. Gran always saw the good in people and things, which was a perspective I really needed. I still need it sometimes.

While I mighta been the only livin' person in Bon Temps who could hear people's thoughts, I sure wasn't the only one goin' home to the kitchen table to get some love. As awful as Maxine Fortenberry could be sometimes, she poured her heart into her ham steak and red-eye gravy when Hoyt was at the table. And Bill said that Russell Edgington's partner, Talbot, threw these crazy banquets at their house in Mississippi, with willing donors and blood ice cream, or somethin' like that. It's creepy, alright, but Talbot and Russell? That was love.

Lately, Jason's been askin' me to fix his meals for him. I think he misses Gran's cookin' maybe even more than I do. Since we've lost Gran, Mama, and Daddy, all we've got left is each other. And the family that eats together, stays together. So as soon as I get all this vampire business sorted out, I got big plans to cook up a buncha recipes that Gran taught me and sit down to a good ole fashioned Stackhouse breakfast.

Life—Over Easy

BY ADELE STACKHOUSE

MAKES 6 SERVINGS

More troubles have been drowned in my sausage and eggs over easy than the whole of Acadiana. For some families, dinner is the time for talkin', but with Sookie at Merlotte's and Jason, well, wherever Jason keeps himself after dark . . . for us, it's breakfast. I remember clear as day that morning after Sookie first mentioned Mr. William Compton. She said the strangest thing: "I can close my eyes and see the farm the pig lived on . . . and even taste the earth the herbs grew out of." What on earth would make the girl say somethin' like that?

Make the sausage: In a large bowl, combine all the ingredients and mix well. Cover with plastic wrap and refrigerate for at least 2 hours.

Roughly chop the mixture (in batches if necessary) in a food processor. Form into 3-inch patties (you should have about 12 patties). Use immediately or wrap in plastic wrap and store in the refrigerator for up to 3 days.

Heat a large skillet or cast-iron griddle over medium heat and cook the sausage patties in batches of four until golden brown and cooked through, turning once, 4 to 5 minutes total. Transfer to paper towels to drain.

Make the eggs: Heat a large nonstick skillet or cast-iron griddle over medium-low heat. Add 1 ½ tablespoons of the bacon fat. When the fat is hot, break three eggs into the skillet and cook until the whites are set around the edges of the yolk, 1 to 1 ½ minutes. With a spatula, gently flip the eggs and cook for about 30 seconds more. Transfer to a plate. Repeat the process with the remaining bacon fat and eggs.

Serve the eggs with the sausage.

Sausage

2 POUNDS	LEAN PORK SHOULDER, CUT INTO 1-INCH CUBES
8 OUNCES	PORK FAT (FROM THE BUTCHER), CUT INTO ½-INCH CUBES
3 TABLESPOONS	CHOPPED GREEN ONION (WHITE AND GREEN PARTS)
1 TABLESPOON	CAJUN OR CREOLE SEASONING MIX
2 TABLESPOONS	SALT
½ TEASPOON	CAYENNE PEPPER
2 TEASPOONS	MINCED GARLIC

Eggs

3 TABLESPOONS	BACON FAT (RENDERED FROM ABOUT 6 SLICES COOKED BACON)
6	LARGE EGGS AT ROOM TEMPERATURE
SALT	
FRESHLY GROUND BLACK PEPPER	

Cracked Eggs Benedict

MAKES 8 SERVINGS

BY BENEDICT "EGGS" TALLEY

Growing up in the Memphis foster care system, I learned to do just about everything for myself. And because I've been smoking pot since I was ten, cooking was always pretty important. Ever since I met up with Maryann and Karl, we've been moving around a lot. When we got to Bon Temps, I saw Tara's people throwing hot sauce and cayenne on the food that gave me my name. Like everything with her, it just feels right.

Boudin Patties

1½ POUNDS	LEAN PORK SHOULDER, CUT INTO 1-INCH CUBES
8 OUNCES	PORK LIVER
¾ CUP	CHOPPED YELLOW ONION
¼ CUP	CHOPPED GREEN BELL PEPPER
¼ CUP	CHOPPED CELERY
SALT	
CAYENNE PEPPER	
FRESHLY GROUND BLACK PEPPER	
¼ CUP	CHOPPED FRESH FLAT-LEAF PARSLEY LEAVES
¼ CUP	CHOPPED GREEN ONION (GREEN PART ONLY)
3 CUPS	COOKED MEDIUM-GRAIN WHITE RICE
¾ CUP	FINE DRY BREAD CRUMBS
1	LARGE EGG
¼ TEASPOON	TABASCO SAUCE
3 TABLESPOONS	PEANUT OIL

Tasso Hollandaise

2	EGG YOLKS
1 TEASPOON	FRESH LEMON JUICE
¼ TEASPOON	SALT
2 TEASPOONS	WATER
½ CUP (1 STICK)	UNSALTED BUTTER, MELTED AND STILL WARM
ABOUT ¼ CUP	FINELY CHOPPED TASSO OR SPICED HAM

Fried Eggs

4 TABLESPOONS	UNSALTED BUTTER
8	LARGE EGGS
CAYENNE PEPPER	FOR GARNISH

CONTINUED

Make the boudin: Put the pork shoulder, liver, yellow onion, bell pepper, celery, 1 teaspoon salt, ¼ teaspoon cayenne, and ¼ teaspoon black pepper in a large, heavy pot. Add water to cover and bring to a boil over high heat. Reduce the heat to medium-low and simmer, uncovered, until the pork shoulder and liver are tender, about 1 hour.

Remove from the heat and drain, reserving ¾ cup of the broth. Let the meat cool and set the broth aside.

Combine the pork shoulder, liver, parsley, and green onion in a food processor. Pulse several times to coarsely chop the meat. Do not purée.

Transfer the meat mixture to a large mixing bowl and add the rice, 1 teaspoon salt, ¾ teaspoon cayenne, and ¼ teaspoon black pepper. Mix well. Add the reserved broth, a little at a time, until the mixture is moist but not gummy. Adjust the seasoning with more salt, cayenne, and black pepper.

Put the bread crumbs in a shallow dish. Combine the egg, Tabasco, and ¼ teaspoon salt in a medium bowl and whisk to blend.

Form the meat mixture into 16 patties, each about 3 inches in diameter. Heat the peanut oil in a large, heavy skillet, preferably cast iron, over medium heat.

Working in batches, dip the patties in the egg mixture, then dredge them in the bread crumbs, coating them evenly. Fry the patties, in batches, in the hot oil until lightly browned, about 2 minutes on each side. Drain on paper towels and keep warm.

Make the hollandaise: In the top of a double boiler or in a heatproof bowl set over a pan of simmering water, whisk the egg yolks with the lemon juice, salt, and water until pale yellow and slightly thickened.

Remove the pot from the heat and, whisking vigorously, add the butter, 1 teaspoon at a time, until all is incorporated. Add the tasso and continue whisking for 30 seconds. Keep the sauce warm in the top of a double boiler or in a heatproof bowl set over a pan of warm water.

Fry the eggs: Melt 2 tablespoons of butter in a large skillet over medium heat. Break four eggs into the skillet and cook until the whites are just set, about 3 minutes. Put each egg on a warmed plate. Repeat the process with the remaining butter and eggs.

Put two boudin patties on each serving plate and spoon over some tasso hollandaise. Sprinkle with cayenne before serving.

Holy Hoecakes

MAKES ABOUT 8 HOECAKES,
2 TO 4 SERVINGS

BY LETTIE MAE DANIELS

Those bottles of booze were just fuel for the demon fire. They kept him alive in me for nearly forty years. But with that exorcism and gettin' myself clean, the Lord ain't never gonna let the demon back into my house. And now that I'm tryin' to rebuild things with my baby girl, I realized Tara hadn't had no hoecakes since her grandmama was alive. I always could make 'em, just never did. Demon never let me. The big secret is you gotta make 'em with bacon grease. It's the only way.

1 CUP	WHITE CORNMEAL
½ TEASPOON	SALT
¾ CUP	BOILING WATER
2 TABLESPOONS	BACON FAT (RENDERED FROM ABOUT 4 SLICES BACON), PLUS MORE AS NEEDED
MAPLE SYRUP OR CANE SYRUP	FOR SERVING

Combine the cornmeal and salt in medium bowl. While stirring constantly with a wooden spoon, pour in the boiling water in a steady stream. Beat until smooth. Let stand a few minutes.

Heat the bacon fat in a large, heavy skillet over medium-high heat. When very hot (but not smoking), reduce the heat to medium-low.

For each hoecake, drop about 2 tablespoons of the cornmeal mixture into the skillet and pat gently into a flat circle, about 4 inches in diameter. Cook several hoecakes at a time until golden brown, about 2 minutes on each side, turning with a wide spatula. Transfer to a plate. If needed, add more bacon fat to the skillet to make the remaining hoecakes.

Drizzle with maple syrup and serve.

Stake and Eggs

MAKES 4 SERVINGS

BY ALCIDE HERVEAUX

I paid off a chunk of my father's debt to Eric Northman when I brought Sookie Stackhouse to Jackson, Mississippi. I 'bout wanted to stake him when I realized what trouble she'd be to actually keep safe. She was out of her mind wanting to go back to the biker bar, so yeah, I was mad when I was makin' her break- fast. Maybe I shouldn't have called her a doormat for runnin' back into the arms of that vamper, but it's hard to feel like a man when I'm cookin' up steak and eggs in a wok.

1 TABLESPOON	VEGETABLE OIL
1	1-POUND SIRLOIN STEAK, ABOUT 1 INCH THICK
CAJUN OR CREOLE SEASONING MIX	
4 TABLESPOONS	UNSALTED BUTTER
8	LARGE EGGS
TABASCO SAUCE	FOR SERVING

Preheat the oven to 350°F.

Heat a large, heavy ovenproof skillet, preferably cast iron, over medium heat until hot, 3 to 4 minutes. Increase the heat to high and add the vegetable oil. Season the steak generously with the seasoning mix. Put the steak in the skillet and cook, turning once, until well browned, about 4 minutes per side. Transfer the steak, still inside the skillet, to the oven and cook for 5 minutes longer for medium-rare.

Transfer the steak to a cutting board. Cover loosely with aluminum foil and let rest for 10 minutes before slicing.

While the steak is resting, heat a large skillet over medium heat, and then add 2 tablespoons of the butter. Break four eggs into the skillet and cook until the whites are just set, about 3 minutes. Transfer the eggs to a plate. Repeat the process with the remaining butter and eggs.

Put two eggs on each plate. Cut the steak on the diagonal into thick slices and arrange on the plates with the eggs. Serve immediately, passing the Tabasco at the table.

Up-in-Arms Biscuits and Gravy

MAKES 8 SERVINGS

BY TERRY BELLEFLEUR

When I came back to Bon Temps from Fallujah, my head wasn't on right. I didn't trust that my kin—Andy, Portia, Grandmama—would be like the boys in my unit, protectin' me when the sun went down. It wasn't 'til I started seein' Arlene that I could sleep the whole night through. The first time I stayed over, I sent Arlene to the couch to rest while I made breakfast for her and for Coby and Lisa. I cooked up the same biscuits and gravy I'd made for my outfit so many times. I couldn't get White Lily in Iraq, of course, so it made me pretty happy to see that there in her cabinet.

Biscuits

2 CUPS	SELF-RISING FLOUR, PREFERABLY WHITE LILY
2 TEASPOONS	SUGAR
½ TEASPOON	SALT
¼ CUP	VEGETABLE SHORTENING
⅔ CUP	WHOLE MILK

MELTED UNSALTED BUTTER FOR BRUSHING (OPTIONAL)

Gravy

1 POUND	BULK BREAKFAST SAUSAGE
¼ CUP	ALL-PURPOSE FLOUR
2 CUPS	WHOLE MILK

SALT

FRESHLY GROUND BLACK PEPPER

Make the biscuits: Preheat the oven to 400°F. Line a baking sheet with parchment paper.

Sift the flour, sugar, and salt into a large bowl. Using a pastry blender or your fingers, cut the shortening into the dry ingredients until the mixture resembles coarse meal. Add the milk and blend it in with a fork until the dough clears the sides of the bowl.

Turn the dough out onto a lightly floured work surface and knead gently two or three times. Roll out the dough to a ½-inch thickness. Using a 2 ½-inch round biscuit cutter, cut out six biscuits. Gather up the scraps, roll them out, and cut out two more biscuits. Set the biscuits on the prepared baking sheet.

Bake the biscuits until golden, 10 to 12 minutes. Brush the tops of the baked biscuits with melted butter if you wish. Leave the biscuits on the baking sheet in a warm place while you make the gravy.

Make the gravy: Cook the sausage in a large, heavy skillet, preferably cast iron, over medium-high heat. When cooked through, transfer to paper towels to drain. Pour off all but 2 tablespoons of the fat in the skillet.

Put the skillet on medium-low heat. Whisk the flour into the fat and cook for 5 minutes, whisking constantly. Remove the pan from the heat and whisk in the milk, a little at a time. Return the pan to the heat, raise the heat to medium-high, and cook, stirring occasionally and scraping the browned bits in the skillet, until the gravy comes to simmer and thickens. Stir in the drained, cooked sausage.

Season the gravy with salt and pepper and serve over the biscuits.

Hopes, Squashed

BY DEBBIE PELT

When Sookie called Alcide to say she was passin' by to see him in Shreveport, he didn't tell her we were back together. He didn't tell her that I had found the program and Jesus. He didn't tell her anything. I tried not to read too much into what he said about how she wouldn't come if she knew he was back with me. After all, it was one of my steps to make amends with her, and I couldn't win back her trust if she didn't show up, right? I made those hostess snacks I used to watch my mama make 'fore all the pack meetings. I'd pickled the squash early on when I was lookin' for a distraction from wantin' V. Sookie didn't take even one bite, the bitch.

6	SMALL YELLOW SQUASH, THINLY SLICED
3	MEDIUM YELLOW ONIONS, THINLY SLICED
¼ TEASPOON	SALT
4 CUPS	CRACKED ICE
2½ CUPS	SUGAR
2½ CUPS	DISTILLED WHITE VINEGAR
¾ TEASPOON	TURMERIC
1½ TEASPOONS	MUSTARD SEEDS
1½ TEASPOONS	CELERY SEEDS

Combine the squash, onions, salt, and ice in a large bowl. Mix gently and let stand for 3 hours. Drain and rinse well in a colander under cold running water. Drain and rinse one more time. Pat the vegetables dry.

Combine the sugar, vinegar, turmeric, mustard seeds, and celery seeds in a large, heavy, nonreactive saucepan over medium-high heat. Stir constantly until the liquid begins to bubble. Remove from the heat immediately.

Pack the squash-onion mixture into clean glass jars or airtight containers and add the hot syrup to cover. Cover and store in the refrigerator for up to 2 weeks.

MAKES ABOUT 4 PINTS

Crawfish Dip

BY SOOKIE STACKHOUSE

I drive all the way to Shreveport to see Alcide, and there's Debbie, with a tray full of hostess snacks? As if crawfish dip is gonna make up for trying to kill me—twice! It would have been nice if Alcide had told me on the phone that she was gonna be there. I'd thought he was just about the only man who was still honest with me. But I suppose he was just tryin' to help his girl. And Debbie did look good, healthy even. I hope she can keep with it. Stranger things have happened.

½ CUP (1 STICK)	UNSALTED BUTTER
1 CUP	CHOPPED YELLOW ONION
½ CUP	CHOPPED GREEN BELL PEPPER
1 TEASPOON	MINCED GARLIC
3 TABLESPOONS	MINCED FRESH FLAT-LEAF PARSLEY
1 POUND	PEELED CRAWFISH TAILS
ONE 8-OUNCE PACKAGE	CREAM CHEESE, AT ROOM TEMPERATURE

SALT

CAYENNE PEPPER

TABASCO SAUCE

PARTY CRACKERS OR TOAST POINTS FOR SERVING

Melt the butter in a large skillet over medium heat. Add the onion and bell pepper and cook, stirring, until the vegetables are soft and golden, 6 to 8 minutes. Add the garlic, parsley, and crawfish tails. Cook, stirring, until the crawfish throw off some of their moisture, 3 to 4 minutes.

Add the cream cheese and reduce the heat to medium-low. Cook, stirring, until the mixture is smooth and heated through. Season with salt, cayenne, and Tabasco.

Serve hot with crackers or toast points.

Beautifully Broken Bisque

BY RUSSELL EDGINGTON

MAKES 4 TO 6 SERVINGS

I may be the oldest vampire walking the earth, but when my one love, Talbot, was alive, he was the master of our house. What care he poured into our collection of Celtic, Norse, and German antiques. He even found those stunning silver doors from the estate of Countess Elizabeth Báthory, Hungary's most famous serial killer. He loved telling guests the story of how she bathed in the blood of virgins. In addition to keeping such a beautiful home, he created the most legendary dinner parties. I ache for Talbot whenever I think of his warm bisque garnished with a flourish of English rose petals.

2 TABLESPOONS	OLIVE OIL
1 CUP	MINCED YELLOW ONION
3 OR 4	MEDIUM BEETS, TRIMMED, PEELED, AND DICED (ABOUT 4 CUPS)
½ CUP	CHOPPED CARROTS
4 CUPS	CHICKEN OR VEGETABLE BROTH
1 CUP	WATER
1 TABLESPOON	FRESH LEMON JUICE
1 TEASPOON	SALT
1 TEASPOON	FRESHLY GROUND BLACK PEPPER
SOUR CREAM	FOR SERVING (OPTIONAL)

Heat the olive oil in a large saucepan over medium-high heat. Add the onion and cook, stirring, until softened, 6 to 8 minutes. Add the beets and carrots and cook, stirring, for 5 minutes. Add the broth, water, lemon juice, salt, and pepper. Bring to a boil, reduce the heat to medium-low, cover the pan, and simmer until the beets are very tender, 20 to 30 minutes.

Remove from the heat and let cool slightly. Using an immersion blender, blend until pureed. (The mixture can also be puréed, in batches, in a food processor.)

Serve warm, garnishing each bowl with a spoonful of sour cream, if you wish.

Cajun Potato Salad

BY ARLENE FOWLER BELLEFLEUR

Oh, I was just sick to my stomach that I brought that Drew Marshall around my friends and my kids. When I found his tape for learnin' how to speak Cajun, well, I just felt so dumb. That man brought nothin' but pain and violence into our lives, coverin' up his crimes with words like cher *and that stupid, sweet smile. But he did leave us with one good thing: potato salad with hot sauce and relish. His Cajun accent may have been fake, but his Cajun cookin'? That was real and good.*

MAKES ABOUT 10 SERVINGS

Potato Salad

1	LARGE EGG
2 TABLESPOONS	FRESH LEMON JUICE
1 CUP	VEGETABLE OIL
PINCH	SUGAR
SALT	
FRESHLY GROUND BLACK PEPPER	
TABASCO SAUCE	
3 TO 4 POUNDS	RED-SKINNED POTATOES, SCRUBBED
8	HARD-BOILED LARGE EGGS, COARSELY CHOPPED

Garnishes (optional)

¼ CUP	MINCED CELERY
¼ CUP	FINELY CHOPPED GREEN ONION (WHITE AND GREEN PARTS)
2 TABLESPOONS	SWEET PICKLE RELISH
2 TABLESPOONS	CHOPPED FRESH FLAT-LEAF PARSLEY

Make the potato salad: Blend the egg and lemon juice in a food processor or blender for 15 seconds. With the processor or blender running, gradually pour in the vegetable oil through the feed tube. The mixture will thicken. Add the sugar, season with salt, pepper, and Tabasco, and pulse to blend. Chill in an airtight container in the refrigerator for at least 1 hour before using. (Since the mayonnaise is made with a raw egg, it's best to use within 24 hours.)

In a large saucepan, boil the potatoes in lightly salted water to cover until fork-tender. Drain and let cool. Peel the potatoes and coarsely chop.

Combine the potatoes and hard-boiled eggs in a large bowl. Season with salt and pepper. Add the mayonnaise and whatever garnishes you wish and toss gently (so as not to break up the potatoes) to mix. Serve immediately or refrigerate until ready to serve.

Candied Sweet Jesus Potatoes

BY THE REVEREND DANIELS

I was so taken by Lettie Mae's testimony that Sunday after her exorcism. I had to know her, to truly understand how the Lord works. I began visiting her, studying the Bible with her to make sure she stayed on the path to righteousness. When she called on me to counsel her daughter, I could see a tenderness had awoken inside her. And when she brought those candied sweet potatoes to the church picnic, well, I had a feeling there was more where that came from. God works in mysterious ways. He had a plan for me: to divorce my wife and marry an even holier soul—and to eat some of the best cooking in Bon Temps.

8	LARGE SWEET POTATOES (ABOUT 3 POUNDS TOTAL), SCRUBBED
½ CUP (1 STICK)	UNSALTED BUTTER, CUT INTO CHIPS
1	LEMON, THINLY SLICED
2 CUPS	WATER
2 CUPS	SUGAR
2 TEASPOONS	VANILLA EXTRACT
2 CUPS	LIGHT CORN SYRUP
1½ TEASPOONS	GROUND CINNAMON

Preheat the oven to 350°F. In a large pot, boil the sweet potatoes in water to cover until tender. Drain and let cool. Peel and cut the potatoes crosswise into ½-inch-thick slices. Arrange the slices in a 3-quart casserole dish. Dot the potatoes with the butter chips. Arrange the lemon slices on top of the butter.

Combine the water, sugar, and vanilla in a small bowl and stir to mix. Pour the mixture over the lemon slices, and then pour the corn syrup over all. Sprinkle with the cinnamon.

Bake until the surfaces of the potatoes are glazed, about 1 hour. Serve warm.

Drop-Dead Tuna-Cheese Casserole

BY MAXINE FORTENBERRY

MAKES 6 SERVINGS

Anyone who knew Adele Stackhouse knew she was just an angel sent from heaven—until of course, she was sent back. Her grand-daughter, on the other hand, is as crazy as a bedbug in a big city. I spent all night after I heard about Adele's passin' makin' my tuna-cheese casserole. But I let it set so darn long, that by the time I'd gotten to the house, they'd cleaned up all the blood. I'd heard they almost cut off her head. Maybe I should have brought my red velvet cake instead.

1 TABLESPOON	UNSALTED BUTTER
½ CUP	CHOPPED YELLOW ONION
½ CUP	CHOPPED GREEN BELL PEPPER
2 TABLESPOONS	ALL-PURPOSE FLOUR
½ CUP	WHOLE MILK
ONE 10¾-OUNCE CAN	CONDENSED CREAM OF MUSHROOM SOUP
TWO 5-OUNCE CANS	TUNA PACKED IN WATER (UNDRAINED)
1 CUP	FROZEN SMALL GREEN PEAS, THAWED
1 TEASPOON	WORCESTERSHIRE SAUCE
SALT	
FRESHLY GROUND BLACK PEPPER	
TABASCO SAUCE	
1 CUP	GRATED CHEDDAR CHEESE
1 CUP	CRUSHED POTATO CHIPS

Preheat the oven to 350°F.

In a large skillet, melt the butter over medium heat. Add the onion and bell pepper and cook, stirring, until the vegetables are soft, 3 to 5 minutes. Add the flour, milk, and condensed soup and cook, stirring, until the mixture thickens. Add the tuna, peas, and Worcestershire and stir to mix. Season with salt, pepper, and Tabasco.

Pour the mixture into a 1 ½-quart casserole dish. Sprinkle with the cheese, and then with the potato chips. Bake until bubbly, about 20 minutes. Serve immediately.

Wipe Away My Red-Eye Gravy over Ham Steak

MAKES 4 SERVINGS

BY JESSICA HAMBY

Pam may have called Hoyt a tree with a plaid shirt, and maybe she was right, but I really loved him. I tried the best I could to be domestic, cleanin' really fast and all, but the cookin'? Can you blame me? Hoyt was always askin' me to make his favorite dishes, the ones his mama used to make. But I didn't know how to make a ham steak with red-eye gravy before I was a vampire, and no way in hell I was gonna learn after the fact. When Mrs. Fortenberry heard we broke up, she sent me the recipe with a note attached: I told you so, evil vamper. *Signed,* Mrs. Fortenberry (a.k.a. Hoyt's mama).

4 SLICES	COUNTRY HAM, EACH ABOUT ¼ INCH THICK
1 CUP	STRONG FRESHLY BREWED BLACK COFFEE
COOKED GRITS	FOR SERVING (OPTIONAL)
FRIED BACON	FOR SERVING (OPTIONAL)

Trim the excess fat from the ham slices and cut the fat into small bits. Put the fat in a heavy, ungreased skillet and fry, stirring frequently, over medium heat until the bits have rendered their fat and become crisp. Discard the bits of fat.

Add the ham slices to the skillet and fry, turning the slices once or twice to brown evenly. Transfer the ham slices to a warm platter and pour the coffee into the skillet. Bring to a boil over high heat, scraping up the browned bits in the bottom of the pan. Boil briskly, uncovered, until the gravy turns red, and then pour it over the ham and serve immediately, preferably with grits and bacon.

Brujo Burger

MAKES 8 SERVINGS

BY LAFAYETTE REYNOLDS

Ain't no one besides Jesus—except maybe my mama—who could get me to cook outside Merlotte's. Every now and again, I'll make him a veggie burger with bacon, if only just to laugh at his silly and cute ass. What a bizarre dude, ordering that just to get a hooker's attention. I tell him every time, "You don't finish that, you ain't gettin' no dessert." Let's just say he's a member of the motherf***in' clean plate club.

⅔ CUP	FINELY GROUND BULGUR WHEAT
¾ TEASPOON	SALT
1 CUP	BOILING WATER
6 TEASPOONS	OLIVE OIL
8 OUNCES	WHITE BUTTON MUSHROOMS, WIPED CLEAN, STEMMED, AND CHOPPED
1½ CUPS	CHOPPED YELLOW ONION
1½ TABLESPOONS	BALSAMIC VINEGAR
¾ CUP	CHOPPED PECANS, TOASTED IN A 350°F OVEN FOR 8 TO 10 MINUTES
1	LARGE EGG, LIGHTLY BEATEN
½ CUP	FINE DRY BREAD CRUMBS
CAYENNE PEPPER	
TABASCO SAUCE	
8	WHOLE-WHEAT HAMBURGER BUNS, WARMED
8 SLICES	BACON, FRIED UNTIL CRISP

Put the bulgur and ¼ teaspoon of the salt in a small heatproof bowl. Pour in the boiling water, stir, and cover. Set aside until the water is absorbed, about 20 minutes. Drain in a sieve, pressing out any excess liquid, and set aside.

Heat 2 teaspoons of the olive oil in a large nonstick skillet over medium heat. Add the mushrooms, onion, and the remaining ½ teaspoon salt. Cook, stirring, until the vegetables are soft, about 8 minutes. Add the vinegar and cook until the vegetables have absorbed the liquid in the skillet, about 2 minutes.

Combine the vegetable mixture and the pecans in a food processor and pulse two or three times to blend. Add the egg and the bulgur and pulse again to blend.

Transfer the mixture to a large mixing bowl and add the bread crumbs. Season with cayenne and Tabasco, and mix well.

With slightly damp hands, form the mixture into eight patties about ½ inch thick. Heat 2 teaspoons of olive oil in a clean, large nonstick skillet over medium heat. Cook the patties in batches of four, for about 4 minutes on each side. Add the remaining 2 teaspoons of oil for the second batch.

Serve the burgers on the buns, topped with the bacon slices.

Sloppy Jason

BY JASON STACKHOUSE

My best friend is askin' for my advice about a girl I can't get out of my mind. Sure, it could be the blood Jessica gave me, but it's also those unbelievable, well, you know, that have me breaking a sweat every time I shut my eyes. When Hoyt comes in sayin' she's slippin' away from him, I don't know if I should be excited or miserable. I cooked him up some sloppy joes, 'cause I couldn't think of anything else to do. I'd rather be cookin' than talkin' anyhow.

1 ½ POUNDS	LEAN GROUND BEEF
½ CUP	CHOPPED YELLOW ONION
1 TEASPOON	MINCED GARLIC
3 TABLESPOONS	RED WINE VINEGAR
1 ¾ CUPS	TOMATO SAUCE
1 TABLESPOON	TOMATO PASTE
2 TABLESPOONS	PACKED LIGHT BROWN SUGAR
SALT	
FRESHLY GROUND BLACK PEPPER	
CAYENNE PEPPER	
6	HAMBURGER BUNS

Preheat the oven to 350°F.

Heat a large skillet over medium-high heat. Add the beef and cook, stirring, until browned, 6 to 8 minutes. Drain the beef on paper towels to remove excess fat. Return the beef to the skillet and add the onion and garlic. Cook, stirring, over medium-high heat until the onion is soft, about 3 minutes.

Reduce the heat to medium and add the vinegar. Cook, stirring to loosen the browned bits on the bottom of the pan, for 1 minute. Add the tomato sauce, tomato paste, and brown sugar and stir to blend. Season with salt, black pepper, and cayenne. Bring to a gentle boil, reduce the heat to medium-low, and simmer, stirring occasionally, for 15 minutes.

Meanwhile, place the buns on a baking sheet and warm in the oven for 5 minutes.

Spoon an equal amount of the beef mixture on the bottom half of each bun and cover with the top half. Serve warm.

Plaisir d'Amour Rabbit Stew

MAKES 4 SERVINGS

BY MARYANN FORRESTER

I see nothing wrong with opening up to love and paying tribute to my master Dionysus. An orgy of debauchery simply allows you to offer yourself to the God Who Comes. Perhaps jealousy, lust, and greed emerge as well, but these are emotions as old as time, as old as me. Orgies always awaken my spirit, so when I slept outside after that night at Sookie's house, I communed with my animal nature. This little fellow hopped by and I thought, mmm, yummy rabbit stew.

1	3-POUND RABBIT, CUT INTO SERVING PIECES
SALT	
CAYENNE PEPPER	
1 TABLESPOON	ALL-PURPOSE FLOUR
¼ CUP	VEGETABLE OIL
4 OUNCES	SLAB BACON, CUT INTO ¼-INCH DICE
1 CUP	CHOPPED YELLOW ONION
1 CUP	COARSELY CHOPPED CARROT
¼ CUP	CHOPPED CELERY
1½ CUPS	CHICKEN BROTH
COOKED LONG-GRAIN RICE	FOR SERVING

Season the rabbit pieces with salt and cayenne, and rub the flour evenly over the meat.

Heat the vegetable oil in a medium, heavy pot, preferably cast iron, over medium-high heat. In batches, add the rabbit pieces and brown them evenly all over. Transfer to a platter and set aside.

Add the bacon to the pot and cook, stirring, over medium-high heat until slightly crisp. Add the onion, carrot, and celery and cook, stirring, until the vegetables are soft and golden, about 10 minutes. Add the broth and stir, loosening the browned bits on the bottom of the pot. Return the rabbit to the pot, cover, and reduce the heat to medium-low. Simmer until the rabbit is fork-tender, about 1 hour.

Adjust the seasoning if necessary.
Serve over rice.

Heaven Scent Pot Roast

MAKES 6 TO 8 SERVINGS

BY LUNA GARZA

I knew better than to let Sam Merlotte come into my life. Marcus wasn't ready to let me be happy. But finding a shifter that my daughter, Emma, could look up to, it just felt worth the risk—not to mention how he made me feel. When he stopped by to apologize for his skin-walker brother, I just couldn't hold a grudge. Marcus always loved my pot roast. I hoped Sam would like it, too. I just didn't expect Marcus to smell it from so far away.

1	4-POUND BONELESS CHUCK ROAST
	SALT
	FRESHLY GROUND BLACK PEPPER
	CAYENNE PEPPER
1 TABLESPOON	ALL-PURPOSE FLOUR
3 TABLESPOONS	VEGETABLE OIL
1½ CUPS	CHOPPED YELLOW ONION
1 TABLESPOON	CHOPPED GARLIC
3 CUPS	BEEF BROTH
12 OUNCES	DARK BEER, SUCH AS ABITA TURBODOG BEER (OPTIONAL)
4	CARROTS, COARSELY CHOPPED
2	BAY LEAVES

Preheat the oven to 350°F.

Generously season the roast with salt, black pepper, and cayenne. Dust evenly with the flour.

Heat the vegetable oil in a large, heavy pot (preferably cast iron) or Dutch oven over medium-high heat. Place the roast in the pot and brown evenly on all sides.

Push the meat to one side. Add the onion and garlic, and stir to loosen any browned bits on the bottom of the pot. Cook, stirring, until the onion and garlic become aromatic, about 2 minutes.

Add the broth and stir again. Put the roast in the center of the pot and arrange the onion-garlic mixture around it. Add the beer (if using), carrots, and bay leaves. Cover the pot with a tight-fitting lid and cook the roast in the oven for 30 minutes.

Reduce the oven temperature to 300°F and cook until the meat is fork-tender, 1½ to 2 hours.

Remove from the roast from the pot and let stand for about 10 minutes. Remove the bay leaves and discard. Skim off any fat that rose to the top of the pan gravy. Slice the roast and serve with the gravy and the vegetables.

What a Fried Chicken

BY SOOKIE STACKHOUSE

I never once got angry and asked "why me, why do I have this, well, disability, and not Jason." But the way he walks around like he's God's gift to women— which I suppose the women of this parish and the three surroundin' it treat him like he is—it burns me up. He even used that charm on Gran, stealin' my favorite fried chicken, right off my plate in front of her, makin' her think it was the cutest thing in the world. I suppose when you look like that, you can get away with anything.

1½ CUPS	ALL-PURPOSE FLOUR
2 TEASPOONS	SALT
1 TEASPOON	SWEET PAPRIKA
1 TEASPOON	FRESHLY GROUND BLACK PEPPER
1 TEASPOON	CAYENNE PEPPER
LARD OR VEGETABLE OIL	FOR DEEP-FRYING
2	3- TO 3½-POUND BROILER-FRYER CHICKENS, CUT INTO SERVING PIECES

MAKES 8 SERVINGS

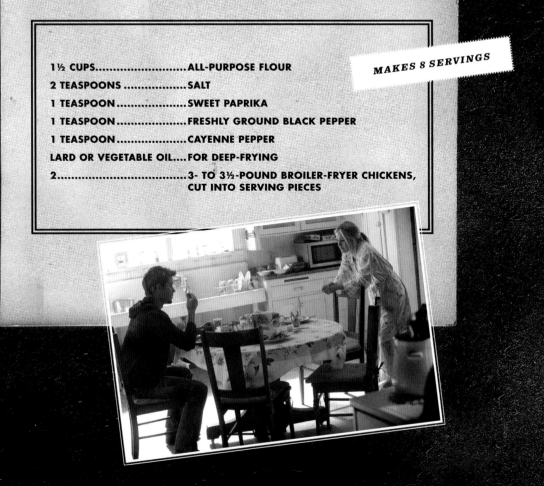

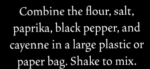

Combine the flour, salt, paprika, black pepper, and cayenne in a large plastic or paper bag. Shake to mix.

Heat about 2 inches of lard until it registers 360°F on a deep-fry thermometer in a large, heavy pot. Put four chicken pieces in the bag and shake well. Add the chicken to the hot fat and deep-fry until golden brown and cooked through, 12 to 15 minutes. Drain the chicken on paper towels. Repeat the process with the remaining chicken. Serve hot or warm.

Corn Bread of Life

BY LAFAYETTE REYNOLDS

That food at Sookie's house when her gran died was just bad juju cookin'. You could smell the fear and nastiness that was comin' off that corn bread from across the cemetery. The way to a man's heart is through his stomach—that sh*t's true as gold. You put some love in your food, folk gonna taste it. After the funeral I brought my own corn bread over to Sookie's house. That bitch is gonna need a lot more than nasty crumbs to help with the grievin'.

2 CUPS	YELLOW CORNMEAL
1 CUP	ALL-PURPOSE FLOUR
1 TABLESPOON PLUS 1 TEASPOON	BAKING POWDER
1 TEASPOON	SALT
1 TEASPOON	SUGAR
1	LARGE EGG, BEATEN
1½ CUPS	WHOLE MILK
3 TABLESPOONS	LARD OR VEGETABLE SHORTENING

Preheat the oven to 400°F.

In a large mixing bowl, combine the cornmeal, flour, baking powder, salt, and sugar. Add the egg and milk and mix well, but do not beat. Heat the lard in a 10-inch ovenproof skillet, preferably cast iron, over medium-high heat until almost smoking. Pour in the batter and cook until the edges begin to turn golden, 3 to 4 minutes.

Transfer the skillet to the oven and bake until the corn bread is golden brown, about 45 minutes. Remove from the oven and let cool for about 5 minutes before cutting into wedges to serve.

MAKES 6 TO 8 SERVINGS

Betrothal Biscuits

BY SUMMER TALLULAH HUCKABY

MAKES 2 PINTS OF JAM AND 10 TO 12 BISCUITS

Jason Stackhouse could see that I was a keeper, telling Hoyt Fortenberry I'd make a great grandma one day. I know I said I'd declare my feelings and then let the chips fall where they may, but I thought the chips would fall in my direction. I baked that man biscuits—my great-gram's recipe, still warm from the oven, butter churned by hand and homemade strawberry preserves, which I picked myself from the church-house garden. I figured once he tasted my biscuits, he wouldn't want anyone else's.

Strawberry Jam

2 CUPS	SUGAR
3 TABLESPOONS	FRESH LEMON JUICE
1½ PINTS	FRESH STRAWBERRIES, HULLED AND HALVED

Biscuits

2 CUPS	ALL-PURPOSE FLOUR
2 TEASPOONS	BAKING POWDER
½ TEASPOON	BAKING SODA
½ TEASPOON	SALT
1 TEASPOON	SUGAR
⅓ CUP	BUTTER-FLAVORED VEGETABLE SHORTENING, CHILLED AND CUT INTO BITS
1 CUP	BUTTERMILK
3 TABLESPOONS	UNSALTED BUTTER, MELTED

Make the jam: Combine the sugar and lemon juice in a medium nonreactive saucepan and cook over low heat, stirring gently, until the sugar dissolves completely, about 10 minutes. Add the strawberries and continue to cook until a small amount of the bubbling mixture gels on a chilled saucer, 10 to 15 minutes. Transfer the jam to clean glass jars or airtight containers and store in the refrigerator for up to 2 weeks.

Make the biscuits: Preheat the oven to 450°F. Line a baking sheet with parchment paper.

Sift the flour, baking powder, baking soda, salt, and sugar four times into a large mixing bowl. Using a pastry blender or your fingers, cut the shortening into the dry ingredients until the mixture resembles coarse meal. Make a well in the center and pour in the buttermilk. Using a fork and beginning in the center, stir until the buttermilk is mixed into the flour. Continue mixing until the dough clears the sides of the bowl.

With floured hands, transfer the dough to a well-floured surface and knead it lightly about eight times, but do not overwork the dough. Pat out the dough to a ½-inch thickness. Cut out the biscuits with a floured 2-inch round biscuit cutter. Gather the scraps, knead together, and cut more biscuits if possible. Arrange the biscuits on the prepared sheet, making sure they just touch each other.

Bake until golden, 10 to 12 minutes. When serving, lightly brush the tops with the melted butter. Serve the biscuits with the strawberry jam.

Confederate Ambrosia

MAKES 8 SERVINGS

BY MAYOR STERLING NORRIS

For the Descendants of the Glorious Dead meeting, my dear Myra made her authentic ambrosia recipe from the 1800s. I sure am proud of her for overlooking her fears and downright distaste for vampires for the sake of the community. She knows how much those meetings mean to the town and to me, given that my great-grandfather fought on behalf of Bon Temps during the Civil War. While she was fiddling in the kitchen, I dug into the town's archives and found that daguerreotype of Mr. Compton's family. When I shared it with him, I swear I saw blood coming out of his eyes where tears might have been.

1	....	**RIPE PINEAPPLE**
5	....	**NAVEL ORANGES**
2 CUPS	....	**SWEETENED SHREDDED COCONUT**
¼ CUP	....	**MARASCHINO CHERRY JUICE (FROM A JAR OF MARASCHINO CHERRIES)**

Trim off the top and bottom of the pineapple. Stand the pineapple on a cut end and, using a chef's knife, cut away the skin. Cut the fruit lengthwise into quarters, and then trim away the woody core from each piece. Cut the pineapple into chunks and drop them into a glass bowl. Add any juices on the cutting board.

Remove the rind and white pith from the oranges. Working over the glass bowl with the pineapple chunks, cut out the orange segments, letting the juices fall into the bowl. Remove any seeds from the segments, and cut the segments in half crosswise. Add to the bowl.

Add the coconut and cherry juice and gently toss together. Cover and refrigerate for at least 2 hours. Serve chilled.

Just Desserts Blood (Orange) Gelato

MAKES 1 QUART, 6 TO 8 SERVINGS

BY TALBOT

Russell loves to say, "It's like Armageddon in here anytime someone chips a dessert glass," but if he knew the effort I put into making our manse as majestic as it is, he'd understand that yes, it is like Armageddon! Do you think Queen Sophie-Anne Leclerq serves a rich gelato with sprigs of delicately cut mint in that tacky New Orleans mansion of hers? Certainly not. She's as mad as a monkey on a tricycle and she has been for centuries! There can only be one lady of the house here, and it's not going to be that spoiled little queen.

1 CUP	FRESH BLOOD ORANGE JUICE (FROM 4 TO 6 ORANGES)
5	EGG YOLKS
½ CUP	SUGAR
2 CUPS	WHOLE MILK
1 CUP	HEAVY CREAM
1 TABLESPOON	GRATED BLOOD ORANGE ZEST
MINT LEAVES	FOR GARNISH

In a small saucepan, bring the orange juice to a simmer over medium-low heat. Continue simmering until the juice reduces by one-third and becomes syrupy, 30 to 40 minutes. Remove from the heat and let cool completely.

Combine the egg yolks with the sugar in a medium bowl and beat with an electric mixer until thick and pale yellow, 4 to 5 minutes. Meanwhile, bring the milk to a gentle simmer in a medium saucepan. Stir about one-half of the warm milk into the egg-sugar mixture (to warm it up so the eggs won't curdle) and whisk to blend. Pour this mixture into the milk remaining in the saucepan.

Cook over low heat, stirring constantly, until thick enough to coat the back of a wooden spoon, 3 to 5 minutes. Remove from the heat and stir in the cream. Strain the custard through a fine-mesh sieve into a glass bowl and cover with plastic wrap, pressing the wrap onto the surface of the mixture to prevent a skin from forming. Chill for at least 2 hours.

Stir the orange syrup into the custard and freeze in an ice-cream machine according to the manufacturer's instructions. Sprinkle with the orange zest and garnish with mint leaves before serving.

Chillin' Out Ice Cream Sundaes

BY SOOKIE STACKHOUSE

Tara comes back from New Orleans, and here I am dealin' with Eric's vampire sh*t. It can't be the home-comin' she was hopin' for. But like she pointed out, there was ice cream, and nothin' screams me and Tara like ice cream sundaes, blankets on the sofa, and cuddlin' up in Gran's livin' room. We've been doin' it since as long as I can remember, and I hope we do it until the day we die.

1 PINT	VANILLA ICE CREAM
2 TABLESPOONS	CRUMBLED PRALINES OR PECAN SHORTBREAD COOKIES
2 TABLESPOONS	CHOPPED FRESH STRAWBERRIES
2 TABLESPOONS	CHOCOLATE SYRUP
¼ CUP	WHIPPED CREAM
TOASTED PECANS	FOR GARNISH

Scoop out about one-third of the ice cream from the carton and eat it.

Add the pralines, strawberries, and chocolate syrup to the ice cream remaining in the carton. Top with the whipped cream and garnish with the pecans.

Grab your best friend, two spoons, and dig in.

Keep from Crumblin' Sugar Pie

MAKES ABOUT
2½ DOZEN CRISPS

BY ADELE STACKHOUSE

Earl's mama taught me to bake leftover piecrust, sprinkled with cinnamon and sugar, and break it into little crisps. Sookie and I would skip the pie and make these just to eat and chat with a cup of coffee in the afternoon. I never could see why someone would pay three dollars for a cup of coffee at a store when the homemade stuff is so much better. Not to mention, you can't get sugar pie at those stores, least not like I make it.

¾ CUP	VEGETABLE SHORTENING
1¼ CUPS	SUGAR
4 CUPS	ALL-PURPOSE FLOUR
1 TABLESPOON PLUS 1 TEASPOON	BAKING POWDER
½ CUP	MILK
2	LARGE EGGS, LIGHTLY BEATEN
1 TEASPOON	VANILLA EXTRACT
2 TABLESPOONS	GROUND CINNAMON

Preheat the oven to 375°F. Line a baking sheet with parchment paper and set aside.

Using a handheld mixer, cream the shortening and 1 cup of the sugar in a large mixing bowl. Combine the flour and baking powder in a medium mixing bowl and stir to blend. Combine the milk, eggs, and vanilla in a small mixing bowl and whisk well. Alternately beat the dry ingredients into the shortening mixture in three additions and the liquid mixture in two additions, beginning and ending with the dry. Stir until the dough comes away from the sides of the bowl.

Flour a work surface and roll out the dough to a ¼-inch thickness. Cut with a 2-inch round cookie cutter and place the rounds on the prepared baking sheet about ½ inch apart.

Combine the remaining ¼ cup sugar with the cinnamon in a small bowl. Sprinkle the rounds evenly with the mixture. Bake until golden, 8 to 10 minutes.

Remove from the oven and cool the crisps on the baking sheet for about 5 minutes before lifting them off. Store in an airtight container for up to 3 days if not serving immediately.

Last Rites Pecan Pie

MAKES ONE 9-INCH PIE, 8 TO 10 SERVINGS

BY TARA THORNTON

Sure, Sookie went a little crazy when that Fortenberry bitch nearly dug into her gran's pecan pie that day before the funeral. But can you blame Sookie? It's the last thing she'll ever eat of her gran's. Everyone needs to stop worryin' about being so damn appropriate. It was hardly an appropriate event. Look at my own mama, standin' up at that funeral thankin' Miss Stackhouse like she goddamn knew her. The only thing she knew was Miss Stackhouse was more of a mother to me than Lettie Mae ever hoped to be.

½ CUP	SUGAR
ROUNDED 1 TABLESPOON	ALL-PURPOSE FLOUR
3	LARGE EGGS
1½ CUPS	DARK CORN SYRUP
1 TEASPOON	VANILLA EXTRACT
1 CUP	COARSELY CHOPPED PECANS
1	9-INCH UNBAKED PIE SHELL, HOMEMADE OR STORE-BOUGHT (THAWED, IF FROZEN)

Preheat the oven to 350°F.

In a small mixing bowl, mix together the sugar and flour. In a large bowl, beat the eggs lightly. Add the sugar mixture to the eggs and stir to blend. Stir in the corn syrup and vanilla and fold in the pecans until well incorporated.

Pour the mixture into the pie shell and bake until the filling is firm and set and the pastry is golden brown, about 45 minutes. Remove from the oven and let cool for about 10 minutes before cutting into wedges and serving.

Seeing Red Bundt Cake

MAKES 1 CAKE, 16 SERVINGS

BY MYRA NORRIS

I was friendly to Adele Stackhouse, just as Sterling had asked. He thought she could help him keep getting reelected mayor since all her friends came out for her meetings of the Descendants of the Glorious Dead. And I was at every one, making my highly regarded desserts. I even showed my respects by bringing my best red Bundt cake to her home. So, is it base of me to point out that she welcomed a vampire into our church? That perhaps her own family was as much to blame for her murder as anyone else? I know it may be less than Christian to point out the ugly truth, but a lie by omission is still a lie and therefore un-Christian, too. What a dilemma!

Cake

½ CUP (1 STICK)	UNSALTED BUTTER, AT ROOM TEMPERATURE
1½ CUPS	SUGAR
2	LARGE EGGS
2 TABLESPOONS	RED FOOD COLORING
2 TABLESPOONS	WATER
1 TEASPOON	VANILLA EXTRACT
2½ CUPS	ALL-PURPOSE FLOUR
¼ CUP	UNSWEETENED COCOA POWDER
1½ TEASPOONS	BAKING POWDER
½ TEASPOON	SALT
1 CUP	BUTTERMILK
1 TEASPOON	BAKING SODA
1 TEASPOON	DISTILLED WHITE VINEGAR

Frosting

ONE 8-OUNCE PACKAGE	CREAM CHEESE, AT ROOM TEMPERATURE
½ CUP (1 STICK)	UNSALTED BUTTER, AT ROOM TEMPERATURE
ONE 1-POUND BOX	CONFECTIONERS' SUGAR
1 TEASPOON	VANILLA EXTRACT

Make the cake: Preheat the oven to 350°F. Grease a Bundt pan with vegetable shortening or butter and sprinkle with flour, shaking out the excess. Set aside.

Beat the butter, sugar, and eggs in a large mixing bowl with an electric mixer on medium speed until light and fluffy, about 5 minutes. Add the food coloring, water, and vanilla and mix well.

Sift the flour, cocoa powder, baking powder, and salt into a medium bowl. Alternately add this mixture, in three additions, and the buttermilk, in two additions, to the buttter-egg mixture, beating on medium speed after each addition.

Combine the baking soda and vinegar in a small bowl and stir into the cake batter, mixing well.

Pour the batter into the prepared Bundt pan and bake until the center of the cake springs back to the touch, 40 to 45 minutes. Remove from the oven and let the cake cool in the pan for about 15 minutes. Invert the cake onto a wire rack and let cool completely.

Make the frosting: Beat the cream cheese and butter in a large mixing bowl with an electric mixer on medium-high speed until fluffy. Gradually add the confectioners' sugar and vanilla and beat until the mixture is smooth.

Gently spread the frosting on the top and sides of the cooled cake. Slice and serve.

Way Back to Joy Banana Pudding

BY SARAH NEWLIN

No, Steve, I do not whip out my banana pudding for just anybody. Jason was special. The Fellowship of the Sun needed him. God needed him. I needed him. Mary Magdalene washed the feet of Jesus and then dried them with her hair. She admired Jesus. She loved him. And she wanted to show him that love. I wanted to show Jason my . . . admiration. Little did I know that my husband was hoping to get the chance to show Jason something, too.

¾ CUP, PLUS 2 TABLESPOONS	SUGAR
¼ CUP	ALL-PURPOSE FLOUR
PINCH	SALT
1 CUP	WHOLE MILK
1 CUP	EVAPORATED MILK
2	LARGE EGGS, SEPARATED
3 TABLESPOONS	UNSALTED BUTTER
1 TEASPOON	VANILLA EXTRACT
ABOUT 20	VANILLA WAFERS
2	BANANAS, PEELED AND SLICED ¼ INCH THICK

MAKES 4 SERVINGS

Preheat the oven to 400°F.

Combine the ¾ cup sugar, the flour, salt, whole milk, evaporated milk, and egg yolks in the top of a double boiler or in a heatproof bowl set over a pan of simmering water. Cook, stirring constantly, until the mixture thickens enough to coat the back of a wooden spoon, 10 to 12 minutes. Remove from the heat and stir in the butter and vanilla.

Layer half of the vanilla wafers, followed by half of the sliced bananas, and then half of the pudding into a 1-quart baking dish. Repeat with the remaining wafers, bananas, and pudding.

In a medium mixing bowl, beat the egg whites with an electric mixer on high speed until soft peaks form. Add the remaining 2 tablespoons sugar and beat until stiff peaks form. Cover the pudding with the beaten egg whites, spreading it to the edge of the dish. Brown the meringue in the oven for 5 to 8 minutes. Let cool slightly before serving.

Totally Surprised Birthday Cake

MAKES ONE 8-INCH LAYER CAKE, 8 TO 10 SERVINGS

BY TARA THORNTON

My birthday always sucks. I'm usually a f***in' mess by the time afternoon comes around, but then Maryann, Karl, and Eggs show up out of nowhere with this huge white cake. Maryann tells me it's all about castin' off the empty shell of what's dead and embracin' the mysteries of what's yet to come. It sounded so good, with that King of Sheba just standing there waiting for me. Maryann said she knew we were going to have a wicked good time that night. If only I had known just how wicked it would all be.

Lemon Filling

¾ CUP	SUGAR
3 TABLESPOONS	CORNSTARCH
¼ TEASPOON	SALT
¾ CUP	WATER
1 TABLESPOON	UNSALTED BUTTER
2 TABLESPOONS	GRATED LEMON ZEST
⅓ CUP	FRESH LEMON JUICE

Berry Topping

1 PINT	FRESH RASPBERRIES
1 PINT	FRESH STRAWBERRIES, HULLED AND SLICED
1 TABLESPOON	SUGAR

CONTINUED

Cake

2½ CUPS	ALL-PURPOSE FLOUR
1½ CUPS	SUGAR
2½ TEASPOONS	BAKING POWDER
½ TEASPOON	SALT
½ CUP	VEGETABLE SHORTENING
1 CUP	WHOLE MILK
1½ TEASPOONS	VANILLA EXTRACT
3	EGG WHITES

Fluffy Frosting

4	EGG WHITES
1 CUP	SUGAR
½ CUP	LIGHT CORN SYRUP
¼ CUP	WATER
2 TEASPOONS	VANILLA EXTRACT

Make the lemon filling: Combine the sugar, cornstarch, and salt in a medium nonreactive saucepan. Gradually stir in the water and bring to a boil, stirring constantly, over medium heat. Cook, stirring, for 1 minute. Remove from the heat and stir in the butter and lemon zest. Gradually whisk in the lemon juice. Let cool completely before using.

Make the berry topping: Put the berries in a bowl and sprinkle with the sugar. Toss gently and let stand for 1 hour or so while you prepare the cake.

Make the cake: Preheat the oven to 350°F. Grease and flour two 8-inch round cake pans.

In a large mixing bowl, blend the flour, sugar, baking powder, and salt. With an electric mixer on medium speed, beat in the shortening, ²⁄₃ cup of the milk, and the vanilla. Beat for 2 minutes, frequently scraping down the sides of the bowl. Add the remaining ¹⁄₃ cup of milk and the egg whites, and beat for 2 minutes more, scraping down the sides of the bowl.

Pour the batter into the prepared pans and bake until the center of each cake springs back when lightly touched, 30 to 35 minutes. Remove from the oven and let cool in the pans for 10 minutes. Remove the cakes from the pans and let cool completely on wire racks.

Make the frosting: Beat the egg whites in a large bowl with an electric mixer until they hold a soft peak. Meanwhile, mix the sugar, corn syrup, and water in a large saucepan and bring to a rolling boil. Cook to 242°F on a candy thermometer, or until a tiny bit of syrup dropped into a bowl of cool water and then pulled between the thumb and forefinger spins a 6- to 8-inch thread. With the mixer running, pour the hot syrup very slowly into the beaten egg whites. Continue beating with the electric mixer until the frosting holds stiff peaks. Beat in the vanilla and use immediately.

Place one of the cake layers upside down on a cake platter and, with a flexible spatula, spread the lemon filling almost to the outer edge. Place the second layer right-side up on the filling.

Frost the sides, bringing the frosting up to form a rim around the edge of the top layer. Spread the frosting evenly over the top, making attractive swirls. Spoon the macerated berries and juice on the top of the cake, allowing the juices to run down the sides. Serve immediately.

MAENAD FEAST

BY MARYANN FORRESTER

||||||||||||||||||||||||||||||||||||||||||||||

When Tara first asked Eggs if I was Satan in a Sunday hat, I couldn't believe how she'd misjudged me. Satan thrives on pain. I thrive on pleasure. When I found Tara, she had nothing. No self-esteem, no home, nobody to love her. She fit beautifully into my little halfway house. I fed off the energy between Tara and Eggs for days. To keep up their strength (and mine), they needed the food of Eros: succulent tropical fruits, Karl's lovingly prepared baked goods, and the occasional hunter's soufflé. And lest they forget about pleasures that my company affords, I throw marvelous parties to remind them that above all, we crave being out of control.

Blood Orange Mimosas

ONE 750-ML BOTTLE .. CHILLED CHAMPAGNE

1 CUP .... FRESH BLOOD ORANGE JUICE

6 MINT SPRIGS .... FOR GARNISH

6 STRAWBERRIES .... FOR GARNISH

Fill each of six flutes with three parts champagne and one part orange juice. Garnish with a mint sprig and a strawberry. Serve immediately.

MAKES 6 SERVINGS

Red Rejuvenating Smoothie

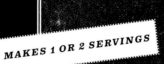

1 CUP	FROZEN STRAWBERRIES
1 CUP	CUBED MANGO
¼ CUP	MILK
¼ CUP	POMEGRANATE JUICE
¼ CUP	VANILLA-FLAVORED PROTEIN POWDER

Combine all the ingredients in an electric blender and blend until smooth. Pour into glasses and serve immediately.

Minty Melon Ball Salad

1½ CUPS	SUGAR
½ CUP	WATER
2 TABLESPOONS	CHOPPED FRESH MINT
¼ CUP	FRESH LIME JUICE
2 CUPS	¾-INCH WATERMELON BALLS
2 CUPS	¾-INCH HONEYDEW MELON BALLS
2 CUPS	¾-INCH CANTALOUPE BALLS

Combine the sugar and water in a small saucepan over medium heat and bring to a boil, stirring to dissolve the sugar. Add the mint leaves and remove from the heat. Let stand for 15 minutes, and then strain through a fine-mesh sieve. Let the syrup cool completely and stir in the lime juice.

In a large bowl, toss the melon balls with the flavored syrup. Cover and refrigerate for at least 2 hours before serving.

MAKES 6 SERVINGS

Ginger-Raspberry Muffins

1 CUP	ALL-PURPOSE FLOUR
1 CUP	YELLOW CORNMEAL
½ CUP	SUGAR
2 TEASPOONS	BAKING POWDER
1 TEASPOON	BAKING SODA
¼ TEASPOON	SALT
1 CUP	BUTTERMILK
¼ CUP	VEGETABLE OIL
1 TEASPOON	VANILLA EXTRACT
1	LARGE EGG
¼ CUP	CHOPPED CANDIED GINGER
1½ CUPS	FRESH RASPBERRIES

Preheat the oven to 400°F. Line a 12-cup muffin pan with paper baking liners.

In a large mixing bowl, combine the flour, cornmeal, sugar, baking powder, baking soda, and salt. Stir to mix.

In a small mixing bowl, whisk together the buttermilk, vegetable oil, vanilla, and egg. Pour into the flour mixture and stir just until the flour is moistened. (The batter will be lumpy.) Fold in the ginger and raspberries.

Spoon the batter into the muffin cup liners and bake until a tester inserted in the muffins comes out clean, 20 to 25 minutes.

Serve the muffins warm.

MAKES 12 MUFFINS

Eating Out
in Bon Temps

GOOD PEOPLE, GOOD EATS

BY SAM MERLOTTE

I never really had a family. Melinda Mickens gave me up while Joe Lee was in prison. Then my adoptive family, if you can call 'em that, abandoned me after witnessin' my first shift. I spent the next nineteen years bein' my own family. Now, I thought the Merlottes were bad people, but hell, the Mickenses made them look like the Brady Bunch. So I like to think that shiftin' is the only part of their DNA that I got. And even though I drifted around for some years, doin' things I ain't too proud of, I finally made a good life for myself here in Bon Temps. At first, I liked it 'cause of the nature and the quiet, but then I really got to know the place. I loved how all the people seemed to know and care about each other. I finally came to understand what havin' neighbors means.

So even though I built this place, it ain't just my bar. It's everybody's. So what if it says "Merlotte's" on the sign? That's just a name. The people that walk through those doors are my family now. They accept who I am. They've got my back. And you know what? I've got their backs, too. This is my town and I ain't runnin' no more.

Now don't get the idea that it's peaches and cream all the time. I worry all the pressure in the kitchen's gonna put Terry back in the VA hospital. Arlene has a conniption fit at least twice a day. I gotta stop Lafayette from mouthin' off to half the customers, even if they deserve it sometimes. Tara, hell, she's always gettin' mixed up in trouble she can't get out of. But truth be told, she's got nothin' on Sookie. That girl is always bringin' around danger worse than I could even think up. All that said, the place wouldn't be the same without 'em.

If you live in Bon Temps, or you're just passin' through, you know you can always break bread here with good people. We got hearts bigger than the size of Texas and the best damn fry cooks in Renard Parish. So as long as you ain't dancin' or talkin' religion, come on down to Merlotte's and make yourself at home.

Skin-Deep Potato Skins

MAKES 6 APPETIZER SERVINGS

BY SOOKIE STACKHOUSE

If I had a order of skins for every guy who had nasty thoughts about me, well, I would have a helluva lotta skins. Before Bill, no one ever thought of me as nice or pretty. It was all about that girl's a freak *or* I'm wantin' to touch this *or* to grab that. *With Bill, it was kinda simple. With Eric, it wasn't so simple. One day he was a scary, mean Viking and the next day, he was a big ole teddy bear. But he never looked at me like I was a freak. As for the guys at Merlotte's? Let's just keep the orders of skins a-comin'.*

6	MEDIUM RUSSET POTATOES, SCRUBBED (ABOUT 3 POUNDS TOTAL)
OLIVE OIL	FOR RUBBING AND BRUSHING ON POTATOES
6 SLICES	BACON, CHOPPED
SALT	
FRESHLY GROUND BLACK PEPPER	
½ CUP	GRATED SHARP CHEDDAR CHEESE
½ CUP	SOUR CREAM
½ CUP	CHOPPED GREEN ONION (WHITE AND GREEN PARTS)

Preheat the oven to 400°F.

Stab the potatoes randomly several times with a sharp, thin knife. Rub them with olive oil and place on a baking sheet. Bake until slightly soft when squeezed, about 45 minutes. Remove from the oven and set aside to cool. Increase the oven temperature to 450°F.

While the potatoes are baking, fry the bacon in a medium skillet over medium-high heat until crisp. Drain on paper towels, let cool, and then crumble. Set aside.

When the potatoes are cool enough to handle, cut each one in half lengthwise and carefully scoop out most of the flesh, leaving about ¼ inch on the skin. (Reserve the scooped potato for another use.)

Put the potato skins on the baking sheet and brush inside and out with olive oil. Sprinkle the insides with salt and pepper. Bake for 10 minutes, flip the skins over, and bake for 10 minutes longer.

Remove from the oven and arrange the skins cut-side up. Sprinkle with equal amounts of the bacon and cheese. Return to the oven and bake until the cheese melts, about 5 minutes.

Top each skin with sour cream and sprinkle with green onion. Serve hot.

Get You Some Wings and Fly Away

BY LAFAYETTE REYNOLDS

Lettin' a vampire bite me? No way. Not even Eddie, the saddest ole man in the goddamn world. Even Lafayette's got some rules, and sex and blood just don't mix in my book. But the night after Sookie and Bill did the nasty for the first time and she had them bite marks on her neck? She was all pornalicious and tangy, just like my fiery chicken wings.

Blue Cheese Sauce

1 CUP	SOUR CREAM
½ CUP	MAYONNAISE
4 OUNCES	CRUMBLED BLUE CHEESE
1 TABLESPOON	FRESH LEMON JUICE
1 TABLESPOON	MINCED SHALLOT
SALT	
CAYENNE PEPPER	
GARLIC POWDER	

Wings

4 DOZEN	CHICKEN WING DRUMETTES (ABOUT 5 POUNDS TOTAL)
1 CUP	TABASCO SAUCE
VEGETABLE OIL	FOR DEEP-FRYING
1 ½ CUPS	ALL-PURPOSE FLOUR
SALT	
FRESHLY GROUND BLACK PEPPER	
GARLIC POWDER	
2	LARGE EGGS
1 TABLESPOON	MILK

2	CARROTS, PEELED AND CUT INTO 3-INCH STICKS
2	CELERY RIBS, STRINGS REMOVED, RIBS CUTS INTO 3-INCH STICKS

Make the sauce: Combine the sour cream, mayonnaise, blue cheese, lemon juice, and shallot in a small bowl and whisk to blend. Season with salt, cayenne, and garlic powder. Cover and refrigerate until ready to use.

Make the wings: Put the wings in a nonreactive bowl and pour in the Tabasco. Toss to coat evenly. Cover and refrigerate for at least 1 hour.

Pour about 2 inches of vegetable oil into a deep, heavy pot and heat the oil until it registers 350°F on a deep-fry thermometer. Meanwhile, put the flour in a shallow dish, season with salt, pepper, and garlic powder. In a shallow bowl, beat the eggs and milk.

In batches, dredge the wings in the flour, shaking off any excess. Dip the wings in the egg wash, letting the excess drip off, and then dredge the wings again in the flour, coating them completely. Fry until golden brown, 4 to 5 minutes. Remove the wings from the oil and drain on paper towels.

Put the wings on a serving platter; put the blue cheese dip, carrots, and celery in bowls; and serve.

Fancy Shrimp Cocktail

BY ARLENE FOWLER BELLEFLEUR

Bless that Terry Bellefleur's heart. Here I am knocked up and he thinks I'm sick on his shrimp cocktail again. The last time, he forgot to put 'em in a cooler, and even if it ain't Fallujah, it's hot as hell on a July night here in Bon Temps. So, yeah, I spent most of that night with my head over the john. But this time? It ain't food poisoning. Just a borin' ole case of morning sickness.

Shrimp

MAKES 6 SERVINGS

4 QUARTS	WATER
2	LEMONS, QUARTERED
3	BAY LEAVES
¼ CUP	SALT
1 TEASPOON	CAYENNE PEPPER
2 POUNDS	HEADLESS JUMBO SHRIMP (21 TO 25 PER POUND)

Cocktail Sauce

1¼ CUPS	KETCHUP
1 TABLESPOON	PREPARED HORSERADISH
2 TEASPOONS	FRESH LEMON JUICE
½ TEASPOON	TABASCO SAUCE
FRESHLY GROUND BLACK PEPPER	

6 LEMON WEDGES	FOR GARNISH
SNIPPED CHIVES	FOR GARNISH

Cook the shrimp: Fill a large pot with the water. Squeeze the juice from the lemon quarters into the water and drop them in. Add the bay leaves, salt, and cayenne. Bring to a boil and add the shrimp. Return the water to a boil and remove from the heat. Cover and let stand for 5 minutes. Drain the shrimp, spread them out on a large platter, and set aside until cool enough to handle.

Peel and devein the shrimp, leaving the tails on. Put the shrimp in a container, cover, and refrigerate for at least 1 hour.

Make the sauce: Combine the ketchup, horseradish, lemon juice, and Tabasco in a small bowl and whisk to blend. Season with black pepper. Cover and refrigerate until ready to serve.

Put an equal amount of the cocktail sauce in each of six small bowls or large martini glasses. Arrange seven or eight shrimp with the head ends in the sauce, and garnish with a lemon wedge and a sprinkle of chives. Serve immediately.

Cryin' in My Hamburger Deluxe

BY JASON STACKHOUSE

I'm tryin' to enjoy my hamburger deluxe when the news comes on and there's Andy—or Detective Bellefleur, as they call him now—goin' on and on about how he's a friggin' hero for shootin' Eggs. Well, I know for a fact that he ain't, and just so nobody finds out, he's gonna make me a cop. He's even gonna enlist his real smart sister Portia to teach me some tricks for passin' the test. Somethin' about keepin' it all in my brain, which sounds weird, but I'll do anything to get that uniform.

Burgers

2¼ POUNDS	LEAN GROUND BEEF
1 TABLESPOON	WORCESTERSHIRE SAUCE
2 TEASPOONS	MINCED GARLIC
2 TEASPOONS	TABASCO SAUCE
SALT	
FRESHLY GROUND BLACK PEPPER	
1½ TABLESPOONS	VEGETABLE OIL

For Serving

6	HAMBURGER BUNS, LIGHTLY TOASTED
MAYONNAISE	
CREOLE MUSTARD	
KETCHUP	
6	TOMATO SLICES
SHREDDED ICEBERG LETTUCE	
EXTRA-HOT (HEADED) FRENCH FRIES (PAGE 171)	

Make the Burgers: In a large mixing bowl, combine the ground beef, Worcestershire, garlic, and Tabasco. Season with salt and pepper. Mix well, but do not overwork. Shape into six patties, each about 4 inches in diameter.

Heat the vegetable oil in a large skillet, preferably cast iron, over medium-high heat. Add the patties, in batches if needed, and cook for 3 minutes on each side for medium-rare, or 5 to 6 minutes on each side for medium-well. (Do not press down on them with a spatula, as that will release all the juices.)

To serve: Spread the buns with mayonnaise, mustard, and ketchup. Put a patty on each, and dress with a tomato slice and lettuce. Accompany with the French fries.

Burning Love BLT

BY AMY BURLEY

MAKES 2 SERVINGS

Want to know why I switched my major from prelaw to philosophy? I had to pursue this theory that finding out your destiny can be transcendent, and that we're all connected. If I hadn't left Wellesley, I would never have found Shreveport or Fangtasia. I wouldn't have met Jason or experienced the amazingness of Bon Temps and its people. And now here I am, serving up BLTs at Merlotte's and kissing Jason in his pickup. It's just what the universe intended. I can't wait to tell the parental units all about it!

6 SLICES	BACON
4 SLICES	WHITE BREAD, TOASTED
4 TABLESPOONS	MAYONNAISE
8	TOMATO SLICES
4	ICEBERG LETTUCE LEAVES

SALT

FRESHLY GROUND BLACK PEPPER

TABASCO SAUCE

In a large skillet, fry the bacon until crisp. Drain on paper towels.

Spread each slice of toasted bread with 1 tablespoon mayonnaise. Pile equal amounts of the bacon, tomatoes, and lettuce on two of the mayo-slathered bread slices. Season with salt and pepper, and top with the remaining toasted bread.

Cut each sandwich in half on a diagonal to serve. Pass the Tabasco at the table.

Melt My Brother's Heart Tuna Melt

BY SOOKIE STACKHOUSE

MAKES 4 SERVINGS

All the girls in this town think Jason's a god, but they know god is just dog spelled backwards. Soon as he gets tired of you, he stops answerin' your calls. Sometimes he even does it to me, and I'm his gosh-darn sister! But Amy doesn't seem nothin' like the girls in this town. Here she is, tellin' me Jason's got so much good in him. Well I've got somethin' to say to her, too: It's gonna take more than servin' my brother your signature tuna melts to keep his attention.

FOUR 5-OUNCE CANS	SOLID WHITE TUNA PACKED IN WATER, DRAINED
¼ CUP	MINCED RED ONION
¼ CUP	MINCED SWEET GHERKINS
2 TABLESPOONS	MINCED RED BELL PEPPER
¼ CUP, PLUS 2 TABLESPOONS	MAYONNAISE
1 TABLESPOON	CREOLE MUSTARD
SALT	
FRESHLY GROUND BLACK PEPPER	
TABASCO SAUCE	
4 THICK SLICES	BREAD, LIGHTLY TOASTED
4 SLICES	PROVOLONE, SWISS, OR CHEDDAR CHEESE

Position a rack about 6 inches from the heat and preheat the broiler.

In a medium mixing bowl, combine the tuna, onion, gherkins, bell pepper, ¼ cup mayonnaise, and the mustard. Season with salt, pepper, and Tabasco. Mix well.

Spread each slice of bread with some of the remaining 2 tablespoons mayonnaise. Spread an equal amount of the tuna mixture on each bread slice. Top with a slice of cheese. Put the open-face sandwiches on a baking sheet and broil until the cheese melts, 4 to 5 minutes. Serve hot.

The Pearl in My Oyster Po' Boy

BY NAOMI

As pissed as I was at Toni, or Tara—whatever I'm supposed to call her—I just wanted her back in New Orleans. So I packed up my car, wrote down the address on that forwarded bill, and drove five hours to that hellhole, Bon Temps. I didn't know what I was going to say when I saw her, but I brought an oyster po' boy with me as a sort of peace offering. It sounds weird, but that was her favorite and I guess I thought I could bribe her back to our place with it. I think I know the real girl underneath all those lies, and if I'm right, she's going to regret not coming with me forever.

24	**FRESHLY SHUCKED OYSTERS, DRAINED**
2 LOAVES	**FRENCH BREAD, EACH ABOUT 10 INCHES LONG**
2 TABLESPOONS	**UNSALTED BUTTER, MELTED**
2 CUPS	**FINELY GROUND YELLOW CORNMEAL**
½ CUP	**ALL-PURPOSE FLOUR**
½ TEASPOON	**SALT**
½ TEASPOON	**FRESHLY GROUND BLACK PEPPER**
½ TEASPOON	**GARLIC POWDER**
¼ TEASPOON	**CAYENNE PEPPER**
VEGETABLE OIL	**FOR DEEP-FRYING**
2 TABLESPOONS	**MAYONNAISE (OPTIONAL)**
8	**TOMATO SLICES**
1 CUP	**SHREDDED ICEBERG LETTUCE**

MAKES 2 SERVINGS

Dry the oysters by patting them with paper towels. Set aside.

Cut the bread loaves in half lengthwise. Brush each half with the melted butter. Set aside.

In a shallow dish, combine the cornmeal, flour, salt, black pepper, garlic powder, and cayenne and stir to blend.

Heat about 2 inches of vegetable oil in a deep, heavy pot or electric fryer until it registers 350°F on a deep-fry thermometer. Working in small batches, dredge the oysters in the flour mixture, shaking off the excess, and then deep-fry in the hot oil until golden brown, about 2 minutes. Transfer the oysters to paper towels to drain.

Spread the mayonnaise (if using) on the buttered sides of the bread. Arrange equal amounts of the fried oysters, tomatoes, and lettuce, in that order, on each bottom half of a loaf. Cover with the top half and serve immediately.

Another Dead Chick-en Sandwich

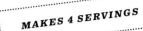
BY ARLENE FOWLER BELLEFLEUR

After Daphne died, all I wanted to do was serve the customers their grilled chicken sandwiches, or whatever, and get on to the next table. But all day long, one customer after another, sick buzzards if you ask me, were wantin' to see the freezer where they found poor Daphne with her heart cut right outta her. Sure, Daphne was clumsy, stupid, and mean, but I wouldn't wish that kinda death on anyone. And anyway, it wasn't a freezer; it was a walk-in refrigerator.

1 TABLESPOON	WORCESTERSHIRE SAUCE
1 TABLESPOON	SOY SAUCE
1 TABLESPOON	WHITE WINE VINEGAR
1 TABLESPOON	TABASCO SAUCE
1 TEASPOON	SALT
½ TEASPOON	CAYENNE PEPPER
½ TEASPOON	GARLIC POWDER
4	BONELESS, SKINLESS CHICKEN BREAST HALVES (ABOUT 6 OUNCES EACH)
4	ONION ROLLS, SPLIT IN HALF AND LIGHTLY TOASTED

MAYONNAISE AND/OR CREOLE MUSTARD

SLICED DILL PICKLES (OPTIONAL)

In a small bowl, combine the Worcestershire, soy sauce, vinegar, Tabasco, salt, cayenne, and garlic powder in a small bowl and whisk to make a marinade.

Arrange the chicken breasts in one layer in a shallow bowl and pour in the marinade, turning the breasts to coat evenly. Cover and refrigerate for at least 1 hour, turning the breasts at 15-minute intervals.

Prepare a grill for a medium-hot fire. Place the breasts on the grill, close the lid, and cook until the juices run clear, 8 to 10 minutes on each side.

Spread the bottom halves of the toasted onion rolls with mayonnaise and top, if desired, with sliced pickles. Place the chicken breasts on top and cover with the top halves of the rolls. Serve immediately.

All Mixed Up Red Beans and Rice

BY SAM MERLOTTE

I was seventeen years old and running scared; could you blame me? My parents abandoned me, I had nothin' to eat and no one to turn to, and no clue what was happenin' to my body. So with my luck, the one house I broke in to was Maryann's. She was sexy as all get out and when she asked me into her bed, hell, of course I went. But you never get somethin' for nothin' in this world, and while she claims to forgive the $100,000 I stole, I just want her to finish up her order, red beans and rice included, and get the hell outta my bar. For good.

1 POUND	DRIED RED KIDNEY BEANS, RINSED AND SORTED
2 TABLESPOONS	BACON FAT OR VEGETABLE OIL
1 CUP	CHOPPED ONION
½ CUP	CHOPPED GREEN BELL PEPPER
½ CUP	CHOPPED CELERY
1 TEASPOON	SALT
½ TEASPOON	CAYENNE PEPPER
¼ TEASPOON	FRESHLY GROUND BLACK PEPPER
2	BAY LEAVES
8 OUNCES	BOILED HAM, CUBED
8 OUNCES	SMOKED SAUSAGE, SUCH AS ANDOUILLE OR KIELBASA, CUT INTO ¼-INCH-THICK SLICES
4 OUNCES	SALT PORK, CHOPPED
COOKED RICE	FOR SERVING
2 TABLESPOONS	MINCED GREEN ONION (GREEN PART ONLY)
2 TABLESPOONS	MINCED FRESH FLAT-LEAF PARSLEY

Put the beans in a bowl and add water to cover by about 2 inches. Let soak overnight at room temperature. Drain the beans and set aside.

Heat the bacon fat in a large, heavy pot over medium-high heat. Add the onion, bell pepper, celery, salt, cayenne, and black pepper and cook, stirring, until the vegetables are soft and golden, 8 to 10 minutes.

Add the bay leaves, ham, sausage, and salt pork, and cook, stirring, until the meat is lightly browned, 5 to 6 minutes. Add the beans and enough water to cover them by about 1 inch. Bring to a boil, reduce the heat to medium-low, and simmer, uncovered, stirring occasionally, until the beans are tender, about 2 hours. Add more water if the mixture becomes dry and thick.

With the back of a wooden spoon, mash about half of the mixture against the side of the pot. Continue to cook, stirring occasionally, until the mixture is creamy and the beans are very soft, 30 to 45 minutes more. Add more water if it becomes too thick. The mixture should be soupy, but not watery. Discard the bay leaves.

Serve the beans over the rice and garnish with green onion and parsley.

Ruby Jean's Hash

MAKES 4 SERVINGS

BY LAFAYETTE REYNOLDS

My mama used to dice up those bells and onions and andouille so fast I thought that bitch was gonna cut her own fingers off at any second. I'd watch her make that damn hot hash with one hand over my eyes, scared stupid, just waitin' for her to say "La La, yo' eggs is ready." Rednecks down at Merlotte's love Ruby Jean's hash. If she knew? She'd tell me to spit in it.

2 TABLESPOONS	VEGETABLE OIL
2 CUPS	DICED COOKED POTATOES
¼ CUP	CHOPPED YELLOW ONION
¼ CUP	CHOPPED GREEN BELL PEPPER
1 CUP	CHOPPED ANDOUILLE SAUSAGE
SALT	
CAYENNE PEPPER	
½ TEASPOON	WHITE DISTILLED VINEGAR
4	LARGE EGGS
2 TABLESPOONS	CHOPPED GREEN ONION (GREEN PART ONLY)

Heat the vegetable oil in a large, heavy skillet, preferably cast iron, over medium heat. Add the potatoes and cook, stirring occasionally, until lightly browned, about 2 minutes. Add the onion, bell pepper, and andouille. Season with salt and cayenne and cook, stirring, for 5 to 6 minutes or until the vegetables are just softened. Remove from the heat.

Fill a medium saucepan with 3 inches of water, add the vinegar, and bring to a boil. Reduce the heat so the water simmers gently. Crack an egg into a cup or small bowl, and gently slide the egg into the water. Repeat the process with the remaining eggs, keeping the water at a gentle simmer. Poach for 3 to 5 minutes, depending on the firmness desired. You can test the doneness by lifting an egg with a slotted spoon and gently pressing a finger on the yolk.

Spoon equal amounts of the hash onto four plates. With a slotted spoon, transfer a poached egg to each serving of hash. Garnish with the green onion and serve immediately.

Extra-Hot (Headed) French Fries

BY ANDY BELLEFLEUR

Now that the world's gone and taken alcohol and V away from me, least they could do is leave me alone with my French fries. But no one ever reckons I'm off the clock, specially at Merlotte's. I earned my spot as sheriff and I do my job like I'm supposed to, but I wish them bloodsuckers would stop raisin' hell in this town so I can enjoy a friggin' meal. It's a goddamned disgrace!

4 OR 5 .... LARGE RUSSET POTATOES (ABOUT 3 POUNDS TOTAL), PEELED AND CUT INTO 3-INCH-LONG STICKS ABOUT ⅜ INCH THICK

VEGETABLE OIL .... FOR DEEP-FRYING

SALT

FRESHLY GROUND BLACK PEPPER

CAYENNE PEPPER

Put the potatoes in a bowl of cool water and let stand for 15 minutes. Drain, rinse under cool water, and pat dry with paper towels.

Heat about 2 inches of oil in a deep, heavy pot or electric fryer until it registers 350°F on a deep-fry thermometer. Fry the potatoes, in batches, until golden brown, about 4 minutes per batch. Remove the potatoes from the pan with a slotted spoon and drain on paper towels. Sprinkle with salt, black pepper, and cayenne. Serve immediately.

The Big O-kra Special

BY ARLENE FOWLER BELLEFLEUR

That scarf Sookie was wearin' was double cute, but there was somethin' different about her. I actually heard her tellin' a customer the okra special was so fresh it'd jump right off his plate. I wanna know what the hell is goin' on with her. She's got access to everyone else's personal business, and I forgive her because she can't help that, but it does make bein' her friend kinda lopsided sometimes. Hopefully it's Sam and not that vampire. Suppose she gets pregnant. How in the world would she nurse a baby with fangs?

⅓ CUP	VEGETABLE OIL
3 POUNDS	OKRA, RINSED, STEMMED, AND CUT CROSSWISE INTO ¼-INCH-THICK SLICES
3 CUPS	CHOPPED YELLOW ONION
1 CUP	CHOPPED CELERY
3 CUPS	CHOPPED, PEELED, AND SEEDED FRESH OR CANNED TOMATOES
1 TABLESPOON	SALT
½ TEASPOON	CAYENNE PEPPER
¾ CUP	WATER OR CHICKEN BROTH

Preheat the oven to 350°F.

Pour the vegetable oil into the bottom of a large roasting pan (not a cast-iron pan, as it will cause the okra to turn black). Add the remaining ingredients and stir to mix well. Cover the roasting pan with a lid. Bake, stirring occasionally, for 30 minutes.

Reduce the oven temperature to 300°F. Continue baking, with the lid on, stirring occasionally, until the slime disappears, 1 ½ to 2 hours. Remove the lid for the last 15 minutes of the cooking time. The time will vary according to the tenderness of the raw okra. Adjust the seasoning and serve.

Runnin' (Onion) Rings 'Round Those Fools

BY LAFAYETTE REYNOLDS

MAKES 6 SERVINGS

Here I am, slavin' over this hot-as-hell grill in this rundown kitchen, and Sam's customers gonna leave my cookin' on their plates? My onion rings are the best damn onion rings in Renard Parish. I don't care where Rene gots to go take Sookie. Finish yo damn meal. These rednecks' palates are as backwoods as they brains.

1 CUP	BUTTERMILK
2	LARGE SWEET ONIONS, PREFERABLY VIDALIA ONIONS, CUT INTO ¼-INCH-THICK SLICES AND SEPARATED INTO RINGS
VEGETABLE OIL	FOR DEEP-FRYING
1½ CUPS	ALL-PURPOSE FLOUR
1½ TEASPOONS	SALT
¼ TEASPOON	CAYENNE PEPPER
¼ TEASPOON	FRESHLY GROUND BLACK PEPPER
¼ TEASPOON	GARLIC POWDER

Pour the buttermilk into a shallow bowl and submerge the onion rings in it. Let sit for 30 minutes.

Heat 2 inches of oil in a deep, heavy pot or electric fryer until it registers 360°F on a deep-fry thermometer.

Put the flour in a shallow bowl and season with the salt, cayenne, black pepper, and garlic powder. In two or three batches, remove the onion rings from the buttermilk, allowing the excess to drip off. Dredge in the flour, coating evenly and shaking off any excess. Fry in the hot oil until golden brown, about 3 minutes per batch. Drain on paper towels. Serve hot.

Coleslaw Comeuppance

BY MAXINE FORTENBERRY

Sam Merlotte never could get a fry cook to make coleslaw as good as mine. But I don't always wanna eat at home: it just reminds me of how that no-good brother of his packed up and left me. After I gave Tommy a roof over his head, food in his belly, and taught the sum-bitch to read, he turned out to be even more disappointin' than Hoyt. Seems like all the men in my life just wanna desert me. Maybe I'll call Summer and see if she wants to join me for dinner tomorrow night.

⅓ CUP	SOUR CREAM
¼ CUP	BUTTERMILK
1 TABLESPOON	CIDER VINEGAR
1 TEASPOON	WORCESTERSHIRE SAUCE
¼ TEASPOON	TABASCO SAUCE
PINCH OR TWO	SUGAR
¼ TEASPOON	CELERY SALT
SALT	
FRESHLY GROUND BLACK PEPPER	
1	SMALL HEAD CABBAGE, FINELY CHOPPED OR GRATED
¼ CUP	FINELY CHOPPED RED ONION
¼ CUP	CHOPPED FRESH FLAT-LEAF PARSLEY
1 TABLESPOON	CHOPPED GREEN ONION (GREEN PART ONLY)

In a small bowl, whisk together the sour cream, buttermilk, vinegar, Worcestershire, Tabasco, sugar, celery salt, salt, and pepper.

In a large bowl, toss the cabbage, onion, parsley, and green onion. Add the dressing and toss to coat evenly. Cover and refrigerate for at least 1 hour before serving.

Did I Kiss Your Grits?

MAKES 6 SERVINGS

BY TERRY BELLEFLEUR

Nothin' worse than Arlene cryin' at me from Merlotte's pass-through window, 'specially when I'm makin' grits. I didn't mean to be peculiar at her. I just couldn't remember what we'd done that night at that Maryann lady's party. The whole town musta been drinkin' too much tequila, because it seems like no one could remember. But I think me 'n' Arlene worked things out, since she promised I'd see her later. I sure am lookin' forward to that.

4 CUPS	WHOLE MILK
¼ TEASPOON	GARLIC POWDER
1 TEASPOON	SALT
¼ TEASPOON	FRESHLY GROUND BLACK PEPPER
¼ TEASPOON	TABASCO SAUCE
1 CUP	WHITE REGULAR GRITS (NOT INSTANT OR QUICK)
4 OUNCES	CREAM CHEESE, CUT INTO CUBES
4 OUNCES	SHARP CHEDDAR CHEESE, GRATED

In a large saucepan over medium-high heat, combine the milk, garlic powder, salt, pepper, and Tabasco. Cook, stirring slowly and constantly, until the milk just comes to a boil. Add the grits and stir to mix. Reduce the heat to low, cover, and cook, stirring occasionally, until the mixture is thick and creamy, 5 to 6 minutes. Add the cream cheese and Cheddar and stir until the cheeses melt completely. Serve warm.

Stuck in My Craw-fish Fritters

MAKES ABOUT 2 DOZEN,
6 TO 8 SERVINGS

BY TOMMY MICKENS

Livin' with Maxine Fortenberry was one pain in the ass after another. There was the preachin', and the babyin', and those stupid dolls. Paid off in the end, though. Wouldn't have been able to fool that gasman if I hadn't been around her enough to get all the details right. Yeah, orderin' two tallboys with tequila shots and crawfish fritters at Merlotte's was more me than her, but since the gasman said he was payin'. . . .

Rémoulade Sauce

¾ CUP	MAYONNAISE
2 TABLESPOONS	KETCHUP
1 TABLESPOON	CREOLE MUSTARD
1½ TEASPOONS	YELLOW MUSTARD
1 TEASPOON	PREPARED HORSERADISH
2 TABLESPOONS	FINELY CHOPPED GREEN ONION (WHITE AND GREEN PARTS)
1 TABLESPOON	FINELY CHOPPED FRESH FLAT-LEAF PARSLEY
1 TABLESPOON	FINELY CHOPPED CELERY
SALT	
FRESHLY GROUND BLACK PEPPER	

Fritters

1	MEDIUM EGGPLANT, PEELED AND CHOPPED INTO ½-INCH PIECES
1½ TEASPOONS	SALT
½ TEASPOON	CAYENNE PEPPER
2 TABLESPOONS	VEGETABLE OIL
½ CUP	CHOPPED YELLOW ONION
8 OUNCES	PEELED CRAWFISH TAILS
3	LARGE EGGS, BEATEN
1½ CUPS	WHOLE MILK
2 TEASPOONS	BAKING POWDER
3¼ CUPS	ALL-PURPOSE FLOUR
4 CUPS	VEGETABLE OIL OR VEGETABLE SHORTENING FOR DEEP FRYING

Fritter Seasoning Mix

⅛ TEASPOON	SALT
⅛ TEASPOON	FRESHLY GROUND BLACK PEPPER
⅛ TEASPOON	CAYENNE PEPPER
⅛ TEASPOON	GARLIC POWDER

Make the sauce: Combine the mayonnaise, ketchup, both mustards, horseradish, green onion, parsley, and celery in a medium bowl and whisk to blend. Season with salt and pepper. Set aside.

Make the seasoning mix: Combine the salt, black pepper, cayenne, and garlic powder in a small bowl.

Make the fritters: Season the eggplant with ½ teaspoon of the salt and ¼ teaspoon of the cayenne. Heat the vegetable oil in a large skillet over medium-high heat. Add the eggplant and cook, stirring, until slightly soft, 2 to 3 minutes. Add the onion and cook, stirring, until soft, 3 to 4 minutes. Add the crawfish and cook, stirring, until they throw off some of their liquid, about 3 minutes. Remove from the heat and set aside to cool.

Combine the eggs, milk, baking powder, remaining 1 teaspoon salt, and remaining ¼ teaspoon cayenne in a medium mixing bowl. Add the flour, ¼ cup at a time, beating with a wooden spoon until the batter is smooth. Fold in the eggplant and crawfish mixture.

Add enough vegetable oil to a deep, large pot or electric fryer to get a depth of about 2 inches and heat over medium-high heat until it registers 360°F on a deep-fry thermometer. Drop the batter, a heaping 1 tablespoon at a time, into the hot oil and fry the fritters in batches. When they rise to the surface, roll them around in the oil to brown them evenly. Drain on paper towels. Sprinkle with the seasoning mix and serve immediately with the rémoulade sauce for dipping or keep the fritters warm in a low oven until ready to serve.

Not-So-Sorry Succotash

BY MARCUS BOZEMAN

It ain't often that she made it, but when Luna cooked up her succotash, I knew it was gonna be a special meal. Hell, that stuff was so good I'da been fine eating only that for dinner. But now that she's shackin' up with a stupid shifter, she better not be makin' it for him. It'll set off my jealous streak . . . and we don't want that to happen, do we?

4 SLICES	BACON, CHOPPED
2 CUPS	FRESH CORN KERNELS (FROM 3 OR 4 EARS)
ONE 10-OUNCE PACKAGE	FROZEN BABY LIMA BEANS, THAWED
½ CUP	SLICED GREEN ONION (WHITE AND GREEN PARTS)
¾ CUP	HEAVY CREAM
¼ CUP	CHICKEN BROTH
SALT	
FRESHLY GROUND BLACK PEPPER	

MAKES 6 SERVINGS

Fry the bacon in a large, heavy
skillet over medium heat until crisp.
Transfer to paper towels to drain. Add the
corn, lima beans, and green onion to the
skillet and cook, stirring, for 2 minutes. Add
the cream and broth and season with salt
and pepper. Reduce the heat to medium-
low and simmer, partially covered, until the
vegetables are very soft and tender, about
15 minutes. Return the bacon to the pot
and adjust the seasonings.
Serve warm.

Bean There, Done That

BY PORTIA BELLEFLEUR

For someone like me with a refined palate, the food options in Bon Temps leave much to be desired. When I'm forced to eat at Merlotte's, I have the one dish that could be called flavorful: onions and green beans prepared with bacon grease. Of course, I simply cannot be eating fried food if I'm going to catch Bill Compton's eye. Bill and I are highly compatible. With him being the King of Louisiana and me practically being Bon Temps royalty, there's no good reason not to form some sort of union, professional or otherwise.

6 SLICES	**BACON**
2 TABLESPOONS	**UNSALTED BUTTER**
1½ CUPS	**CHOPPED YELLOW ONION**
1 POUND	**FRESH GREEN BEANS, TRIMMED**
2 CUPS	**WATER OR CHICKEN BROTH**
8 OUNCES	**TASSO OR SMOKED HAM, CHOPPED**
SALT	
FRESHLY GROUND BLACK PEPPER	

In a large skillet, fry the bacon over medium heat until crisp. Transfer to paper towels to drain, and set aside.

Add the butter to the skillet with the bacon drippings, still over medium heat. When the butter has melted, add the onion and cook, stirring, until the onion is soft and golden, about 10 minutes. Add the green beans, water, and tasso and season with salt and pepper. Bring to a boil, and reduce the heat to medium-low. Cover the skillet and simmer, stirring occasionally, until the beans are completely tender, about 45 minutes. Uncover and continue simmering until most of the liquid has evaporated, about 45 minutes. Adjust the seasoning.

Crumble the reserved bacon and sprinkle it over the beans. Serve hot.

A Hush-ed Puppy

BY MARYANN FORRESTER

Poor Sam. He's so worried that "his people" in "his bar" in "his town" are somehow going to get hurt while they're simply submitting to all their most natural urges. So what? They're drinking, dancing, and nearly having sex on the pool table. They're enjoying themselves—something that Sam doesn't really know how to do. It's a shame. Someone who makes hush puppies this good should know a thing or two about getting down and dirty.

¼ CUP	ALL-PURPOSE FLOUR
1 TABLESPOON PLUS 1 TEASPOON	DOUBLE-ACTING BAKING POWDER
½ TEASPOON	SALT
1½ CUPS	WHITE CORNMEAL
2	LARGE EGGS
¾ TO 1 CUP	BUTTERMILK
1 TABLESPOON	FINELY CHOPPED GREEN ONION (WHITE PART ONLY)
1 TEASPOON	MINCED GARLIC
LARD OR VEGETABLE OIL	FOR DEEP-FRYING
SALT AND FRESHLY GROUND BLACK PEPPER FOR DUSTING (OPTIONAL)	

Combine the flour, baking powder, and salt and sift them into a large mixing bowl. Add the cornmeal and stir to blend. Add the eggs, one a time, beating well with a wooden spoon until the mixture is smooth.

Pour in ¾ cup of the buttermilk and stir until it is completely absorbed. If the batter is dense and thick, add more buttermilk, 1 tablespoon at a time, until the batter holds its shape in a spoon. Add the green onion and garlic, and stir to blend.

Melt enough lard to get a depth of about 2 inches in a deep, heavy pot or electric fryer and heat until it registers 360°F on a deep-fry thermometer. Scoop rounded tablespoons of the batter and drop, four or five at a time, into the hot oil. Fry, turning, to brown evenly, about 3 minutes. Drain on paper towels. While hot, dust the hush puppies with salt and pepper if you wish. Keep warm in a low oven while you fry the rest. Serve warm.

Boilin' Over Engagement Party

BY HOYT FORTENBERRY

MAKES 4 TO 6 SERVINGS

Jason's had hisself plenty of lookers. Rene got engaged to Arlene, who I think is still pretty hot even though she's a mom and all. But who do I got talkin' at me over this crawfish boil? My gosh-darned mama, tellin' me how many beers I can drink and askin' me to get extra crawfish with all the fixin's for her. Well I've had it with takin' orders from Mama. If I want to have six beers and enough tequila to drown a Mexican sea captain, I'm gonna do it, even if I'm gonna be hurtin' tomorrow.

Dip

2 CUPS	MAYONNAISE
½ CUP	KETCHUP
2 TEASPOONS	PREPARED HORSERADISH
2 TEASPOONS	WORCESTERSHIRE SAUCE
2 TEASPOONS	FRESH LEMON JUICE
½ TEASPOON	TABASCO SAUCE

Crawfish Boil

2 CUPS	SALT
½ CUP	CAYENNE PEPPER
4 TO 6	MEDIUM RED-SKINNED POTATOES
4 TO 6	MEDIUM YELLOW ONIONS
3 OR 4	LEMONS, HALVED
1	LARGE HEAD GARLIC, HALVED CROSSWISE
3 EARS	FRESH CORN, SHUCKED AND HALVED
12 POUNDS	LIVE CRAWFISH

Make the dip: Combine all of the ingredients in a mixing bowl and whisk well. Store in an airtight container in the refrigerator until ready to serve.

Make the crawfish boil: In a small bowl, combine the salt and cayenne to make a seasoning mix. In a large boiling pot, pour in 5 gallons of water. Add the seasoning mix, potatoes, onions, lemons, and garlic. Bring to a boil, cover, and boil for about 20 minutes. Add the corn and crawfish. Cover the pot, return to a boil, and continue boiling for 2 minutes. Remove from the heat and let stand, covered, for 15 minutes. Drain.

Serve the crawfish boil on a newspaper-covered table or on large trays with the dip.

Gumbo Ya Ya

MAKES ABOUT 8 SERVINGS

BY LAFAYETTE REYNOLDS

People come from all over to eat my gumbo. Sometimes one of 'em will catch me on the way outta work and ask what my "secret" is. I tell 'em, "Hooker, if I tell you the secret, how's I'm gonna get yo ass back to Merlotte's for more?" Truth is, there ain't much of a secret that any of those bitches can do anything about. It's all in the wrist—I gotta gift for slicing those peppers so fine, they practically melt in the pot. And that's somethin' you either got or you don't.

1	4- TO 5-POUND WHOLE CHICKEN, CUT INTO SERVING PIECES
SALT	
CAYENNE PEPPER	
1 CUP	VEGETABLE OIL
1 CUP	ALL-PURPOSE FLOUR
2 CUPS	CHOPPED ONION
1 CUP	CHOPPED BELL PEPPER
½ CUP	CHOPPED CELERY
ABOUT 10 CUPS	CHICKEN BROTH
2	BAY LEAVES
½ TEASPOON	DRIED THYME LEAVES
1 POUND	ANDOUILLE SAUSAGE, CUT CROSSWISE INTO ¼-INCH-THICK SLICES
¼ CUP	CHOPPED GREEN ONION (GREEN PART ONLY)
2 TABLESPOONS	CHOPPED FRESH FLAT-LEAF PARSLEY
HOT COOKED RICE	FOR SERVING
FILÉ POWDER (OPTIONAL)	

Season the chicken generously with salt and cayenne. Set aside.

In a large, heavy pot or Dutch oven, combine the vegetable oil and flour over medium heat. Cook, stirring constantly, until the roux is dark brown, 25 to 30 minutes. Add the onion, bell pepper, and celery and cook, stirring, until very soft, 10 to 12 minutes. Add the broth and stir to blend well. Add the chicken, bay leaves, and thyme. Bring to a boil, reduce the heat to medium-low, and simmer, partially covered, until the chicken is very tender, 2 to 3 hours.

Add the andouille and cook for 30 minutes. Adjust the seasonings. Discard the bay leaves and add the green onion and parsley. Put some rice into each soup bowl, and spoon some gumbo on top to serve. Pass the filé powder at the table, if you like.

Chicken-Fried Love with Gravy

BY JESSICA HAMBY

The first time I met Hoyt, he went on and on about crispy chicken-'n'-steak babies. It was real cute, how nervous he got. So when me 'n' him moved in together, I snagged Lafayette's recipe from Merlotte's. I figured Hoyt was so good to me that maybe I'd return the favor and cook it for him someday. Never could build up the nerve to do it though, 'cause human food makes me retch. So instead, whenever I wanna show him how much I care, I just take him back to that same ole booth and get him a double order of the chicken-fried steak.

MAKES 4 SERVINGS

Chicken-Fried Steak

FOUR 6-OUNCE PIECES	CUBED STEAK
SALT	
FRESHLY GROUND BLACK PEPPER	
CAYENNE PEPPER	
1½ CUPS	ALL-PURPOSE FLOUR
2	LARGE EGGS
1 CUP	BUTTERMILK
2 CUPS	VEGETABLE OIL

Cream Gravy

5 TABLESPOONS	UNSALTED BUTTER
¼ CUP PLUS 1 TABLESPOON	ALL-PURPOSE FLOUR
2½ CUPS	WHOLE MILK
SALT	
COARSELY GROUND BLACK PEPPER	
CAYENNE PEPPER	

Make the chicken-fried steak: Generously season the meat with salt, black pepper, and cayenne. Put the flour in a shallow dish and season with salt, black pepper, and cayenne. Put the eggs and the buttermilk in another shallow bowl and whisk well to blend.

In a large, heavy skillet, preferably cast iron, heat the vegetable oil until it registers 350°F on a deep-fry thermometer.

Dredge two pieces of meat first in the seasoned flour, then in the egg mixture, then again in the flour, coating them evenly and pressing the flour into the meat with the heel of your hand. Fry in the hot oil until crisp and golden brown, about 5 minutes per side. Drain the meat on paper towels and keep warm while your repeat the process with the remaining two pieces of meat.

Make the gravy: While the steak is frying, melt the butter in a large skillet over medium-high heat. Whisk in the flour and cook, stirring slowly and constantly, until the mixture is smooth and light brown, 4 to 5 minutes.

Reduce the heat to medium-low and slowly whisk in the milk. Cook, whisking constantly, until the mixture is smooth and thick, 8 to 10 minutes. Season with salt, black pepper, and cayenne.

Serve the chicken-fried steaks smothered with the gravy.

I Wanna Snapper in Two

BY SOOKIE STACKHOUSE

That Maryann woman just about ate everything we got here at Merlotte's. She even ordered the stuffed snapper with crawfish dressing, which I don't think anyone's ordered in, like, three years. Sam was threatenin' to take it off the menu but Lafayette insisted he keep it on there. It is pretty dang delicious. But how in heck she eats that much without having a heart attack or gettin' fat is beyond me. I just hope that her bad habits aren't rubbin' off on Tara.

Stuffed Snapper

1	8-POUND RED SNAPPER, SCALED AND GUTTED, WITH HEAD AND TAIL LEFT ON
	SALT
	CAYENNE PEPPER
¾ CUP (1½ STICKS)	UNSALTED BUTTER
1 CUP	FINELY CHOPPED YELLOW ONION
½ CUP	FINELY CHOPPED CELERY
½ CUP	FINELY CHOPPED GREEN BELL PEPPER
2	GARLIC CLOVES, MINCED
1 POUND	SMALL SHRIMP (51 TO 60 PER POUND), PEELED AND DEVEINED
1 POUND	LUMP CRABMEAT, PICKED OVER FOR SHELLS AND CARTILAGE
PINCH	DRIED OREGANO
PINCH	DRIED THYME
1	LARGE EGG
1½ CUPS	FINE DRIED BREAD CRUMBS
3 TABLESPOONS	OLIVE OIL
¼ CUP	FRESH LEMON JUICE

CONTINUED

Crawfish Topping

½ CUP (1 STICK) .... UNSALTED BUTTER

3 TABLESPOONS .... ALL-PURPOSE FLOUR

1 CUP .... WHOLE MILK OR
HALF-AND-HALF

1 CUP .... FINELY CHOPPED
GREEN ONION
(GREEN PART ONLY)

1 POUND .... PEELED CRAWFISH
TAILS

3 .... GARLIC CLOVES,
MINCED

SALT

FRESHLY GROUND WHITE PEPPER

2 TABLESPOONS .... MINCED FRESH
FLAT-LEAF PARSLEY

½ CUP .... DRY WHITE WINE

2 TABLESPOONS .... TOMATO PASTE

LEMON SLICES .... FOR GARNISH

OLIVES..................... TO PUT IN THE EYES
OF THE SNAPPER

Make the stuffed snapper: Preheat the oven to 400°F. Rub the fish well both inside and out with salt and cayenne. Set aside.

In a large skillet, melt ½ cup of the butter over medium heat. Add the onion, celery, bell pepper, and garlic and cook, stirring, until the vegetables are soft, about 4 minutes. Add the shrimp and cook until they turn pink. Add the crabmeat and toss gently. Stir in the oregano and thyme and season with salt and cayenne. Add the egg and stir. Add the bread crumbs, a little at a time, to bind the mixture. Let cool to room temperature. Meanwhile, melt the remaining 4 tablespoons butter.

Fill the cavity of the fish with the stuffing and secure with toothpicks. Set the fish in a large baking dish. In a small bowl, combine the melted butter with the olive oil and lemon juice, and baste the fish with this mixture.

Bake the fish for 15 minutes and then baste again with lemon-butter mixture. Reduce the oven temperature to 350°F and continue to bake for about 45 minutes more, or until the fish flakes easily with a fork.

Make the crawfish topping: While the fish is baking, melt 4 tablespoons of the butter in a heavy saucepan over medium heat. Add the flour and whisk to blend. Slowly add the milk and cook, stirring, until you have a slightly thickened sauce, about 10 minutes. Remove from the heat and set aside.

Melt the remaining 4 tablespoons butter in a large skillet over medium heat. Add the green onion and crawfish tails and cook, stirring, until the onion is softened and the crawfish throws off a little liquid, 3 to 4 minutes. Add the garlic, season with salt and white pepper, and add the parsley. Simmer for 2 minutes. Add the crawfish mixture to the sauce in the saucepan and cook over medium heat, stirring to blend. Stir in the wine and tomato paste. Adjust the seasoning with salt and white pepper and continue to simmer, stirring occasionally, until the sauce is thick enough to coat the back of a spoon, about 4 minutes.

Transfer the fish to a serving platter. Garnish with the lemon slices and put olives in the eye sockets. Remove the toothpicks. Arrange a heaping tablespoonful of stuffing and a few pieces of fish on each of eight plates, and spoon the crawfish topping over the fish. Serve immediately.

Blackened (Rib-)Eye

BY TARA THORNTON

MAKES 4 SERVINGS

I'm sort of a blackout expert. Had to be, with the mama I had. She was always wakin' up with no clue where she'd been or who with. And now I have the same drama in my life. Wakin' up with Eggs, both of us beaten to hell, but neither of us rememberin' a damn thing about the night before. We went to Merlotte's so he could get lunch while I worked. Eggs made a joke about needin' a rib-eye for his rib and for my eye. It was kind of funny until Lafayette showed up and started screamin' and makin' a big deal about it.

1 TABLESPOON	SALT
1 TABLESPOON	CHILI POWDER
2 TEASPOONS	DRIED THYME LEAVES
1 TEASPOON	CAYENNE PEPPER
1 TEASPOON	FRESHLY GROUND BLACK PEPPER
½ TEASPOON	GARLIC POWDER
¼ TEASPOON	ONION POWDER
4	12-OUNCE BONELESS RIB-EYE STEAKS (EACH 1 INCH THICK), AT ROOM TEMPERATURE
4 TABLESPOONS	BUTTER, AT ROOM TEMPERATURE

In a small bowl, combine the salt, chili powder, dried thyme, cayenne, black pepper, garlic powder, and onion powder and stir to blend.

Heat two large cast-iron skillets over high heat until very hot. Brush one side of each steak with ½ tablespoon butter and sprinkle with about 1 ½ teaspoons of the spice blend. Place two steaks, seasoned-side down, in each skillet. Brush the tops with ½ tablespoon butter and sprinkle with 1 ½ teaspoons of the spice blend. Cook for about 2 minutes on each side for medium-rare (about 135°F on an instant-read thermometer), or to the desired doneness. (If you have only one large cast iron skillet, cook the steaks two at a time and tent the first batch with aluminum foil while you cook the second batch.) Serve immediately.

Smothered (My Boys) Pork Chops

BY MELINDA MICKENS

It broke my heart that my oldest boy kicked me outta his life. He spent so long lookin' for me, but then we were only together for a hot minute when BAM! Back out on the streets. We had it real good with him, too! Not havin' to go to the dog fights, bein' treated like a real human bein', eatin' everything on the house just cause I was his mama. 'Specially liked those smothered pork chops. Wish I could say I taught him how to make 'em, but we all know that ain't true.

8	6-OUNCE BONE-IN PORK CHOPS (EACH 1½ INCHES THICK)
1 TEASPOON	SALT
½ TEASPOON	CAYENNE PEPPER
¼ TEASPOON	FRESHLY GROUND BLACK PEPPER
½ CUP	ALL-PURPOSE FLOUR
¼ CUP	VEGETABLE OIL
¾ CUP	WATER, PLUS MORE AS NEEDED
2	MEDIUM YELLOW ONIONS, THINLY SLICED AND SEPARATED INTO RINGS
COOKED RICE	FOR SERVING (OPTIONAL)

Season the pork chops with the salt, cayenne, and black pepper. Put the flour in a shallow dish and dredge the pork chops, coating both sides evenly.

Heat the vegetable oil in a large, heavy skillet over medium-high heat. Brown the pork chops evenly on both sides in batches. Return all the pork chops to the pan, add ½ cup of the water, and cover the pan. Reduce the heat to medium-low and simmer until the pork chops are tender, about 30 minutes. Transfer the pork chops to a platter.

Add the onions to the skillet and cook, stirring, until soft and lightly browned, 10 to 15 minutes. Add the remaining ¼ cup water and stir to loosen any browned bits on the bottom of the pan. (You may have to add about another ¼ cup water if the mixture is very dry.) Return the pork chops to the pan. Cover and simmer for 30 minutes or until the chops are firm—but not taut—when pressed with a fingertip.

Serve the pork chops and onions over rice if you wish.

What a Jam-balaya

BY HOLLY CLEARY

Andy was real nice askin' me out. And he was nervous, too, which means that he's really sweet on the inside. But like everyone, he's not all of one thing or another. We're all mixes of our wants, our needs, our futures, and our pasts. If Andy were a food, he'd be like a hearty stew. And if I were a food, I'd be vegetarian jambalaya. Good for ya, but with a little spice thrown in.

3 TABLESPOONS	VEGETABLE OIL
12 OUNCES	PORK TENDERLOIN, TRIMMED AND CUT INTO ½-INCH DICE
12 OUNCES	BOILED HAM, CUT INTO ½-INCH DICE
12 OUNCES	SMOKED SAUSAGE, CUT CROSSWISE INTO ¼-INCH-THICK SLICES
¼ CUP PLUS 1 TABLESPOON	BACON FAT (RENDERED FROM 9 TO 10 SLICES BACON)
1¼ CUPS	CHOPPED YELLOW ONION
½ CUP	CHOPPED GREEN BELL PEPPER
1 CUP	CHOPPED CELERY
1 TEASPOON	CHOPPED GARLIC
4 CUPS	CHICKEN BROTH
½ CUP	CHOPPED GREEN ONION (GREEN PART ONLY)
2 CUPS	LONG-GRAIN RICE
ONE 14½-OUNCE CAN	DICED TOMATOES, DRAINED
¼ CUP	CHOPPED FRESH FLAT-LEAF PARSLEY
2	BAY LEAVES
SALT	
CAYENNE PEPPER	

Preheat the oven to 350°F.

In a large, heavy, ovenproof pot with a tight-fitting lid, such as a Dutch oven, heat the vegetable oil over medium-high heat and add the pork, ham, and sausage. Cook, stirring, until the meats are browned evenly, 8 to 10 minutes. Transfer to a platter and pour off the oil.

Return the pot to medium heat. Add the bacon fat, onion, bell pepper, celery, and garlic and cook until soft and pale gold, 8 to 10 minutes. Add the broth, green onion, rice, tomatoes, parsley, and bay leaves. Season generously with salt and cayenne, and stir to mix well.

Cover the pot and transfer to the oven. Bake until the rice is tender and has absorbed all the liquid, about 1 hour. Uncover and stir gently with a fork. (If the rice is too moist, reduce the oven temperature to 225°F, return the pot, uncovered, to the oven, and cook for 10 to 15 minutes longer, or until the rice is drier.) Let stand for about 10 minutes before serving.

Gone to the Dogs Catfish

BY ALCIDE HERVEAUX

'Fore I got my courage up to talk to Sookie, I sat at the bar at Merlotte's eatin' fried catfish and thinkin' about that thing people say: "Follow your heart." Well, what those people don't realize is that sometimes your heart can make you do the same stupid thing over and over again. Followin' my heart led me to Debbie. It led Sookie to Bill, and then to Eric Northman. Maybe me 'n' Sookie need to start ignorin' our hearts and listenin' to our brains a little more.

MAKES ABOUT 4 SERVINGS

Tartar Sauce

1 CUP	MAYONNAISE
1 TABLESPOON	CREOLE MUSTARD
1 TABLESPOON	CHOPPED FRESH FLAT-LEAF PARSLEY
1 TABLESPOON	CHOPPED GREEN ONION (GREEN PART ONLY)
1 TEASPOON	CHOPPED GARLIC
¼ TEASPOON	TABASCO SAUCE
SALT	
FRESHLY GROUND BLACK PEPPER	

Fish

1½ POUNDS	CATFISH FILLETS, CUT INTO 1-BY-3-INCH STRIPS
1 TEASPOON	SALT
½ TEASPOON	CAYENNE PEPPER
1 CUP	WHOLE MILK
2 TABLESPOONS	YELLOW MUSTARD
2 TABLESPOONS	FRESH LEMON JUICE
3 OR 4 DASHES	TABASCO SAUCE
2 CUPS	FINELY GROUND YELLOW CORNMEAL
1 TABLESPOON	CORNSTARCH
VEGETABLE OIL OR VEGETABLE SHORTENING FOR DEEP-FRYING	

1	LARGE YELLOW ONION, THINLY SLICED AND SEPARATED INTO RINGS

Make the tartar sauce: Combine the mayonnaise, mustard, parsley, green onion, garlic, and Tabasco in a small mixing bowl and blend well. Season with salt and pepper. Refrigerate for at least 1 hour before serving.

Make the fish: Season the fish with the salt and cayenne. Put in a nonreactive bowl and add the milk, mustard, lemon juice, and Tabasco. Cover and refrigerate for at least 1 hour.

Put the cornmeal and cornstarch into a brown paper bag. Remove the catfish from the marinade, a few pieces at a time, allowing the marinade to drip off a bit. Put the strips in the bag and shake well to coat each piece.

Add enough vegetable oil to a deep, heavy pot or electric fryer to get a depth of about 2 inches and heat over medium-high heat until it registers 360°F on a deep-fry thermometer. Drop a few pieces of fish at a time into the hot oil. When they rise to the surface and are golden brown, remove and drain on paper towels.

Scatter the onions over the fish and serve with the tartar sauce.

Jailhouse Chili

MAKES 8 SERVINGS

BY TERRY BELLEFLEUR

Sam lets us bring in a lot of ideas for recipes and stuff, so I came up with something called "jailhouse chili," a dish that I learned about during basic training. There's one critical ingredient: corn chips. Without it you don't have jailhouse chili. You got just a messy scramble of stuff. The corn chips bring it all together into one of the more popular dishes here at Merlotte's, if I do say so myself.

1 ½ POUNDS	COARSELY GROUND BEEF
½ POUND	COARSELY GROUND PORK
3 TABLESPOONS	VEGETABLE OIL
1 CUP	CHOPPED YELLOW ONION
2	JALAPEÑO CHILES, SEEDED AND CHOPPED
TWO 15-OUNCE CANS	RED KIDNEY BEANS
2 CUPS	CANNED DICED TOMATOES WITH THEIR JUICES
ONE 6-OUNCE CAN	TOMATO PASTE
2 TO 3 TABLESPOONS	CHILI POWDER
SALT	
CAYENNE PEPPER	
WATER OR BEEF BROTH, AS NEEDED	
SHREDDED CHEDDAR CHEESE	FOR SERVING
CRUSHED CORN CHIPS	FOR SERVING
TABASCO SAUCE	FOR SERVING

Combine the ground meats in a medium bowl and mix well. Heat the vegetable oil in a large, heavy pot or Dutch oven over medium-high heat. Brown the meat mixture in the pot until all the pink has disappeared. Add the onion and jalapeños and cook, stirring occasionally, for 10 minutes, or until the onion is softened. Add the kidney beans, tomatoes, and tomato paste. Add 2 tablespoons chili powder for a mild-tasting dish or 3 tablespoons for a more assertive one and season with salt and cayenne. Reduce the heat to medium-low and simmer uncovered for 1 ½ hours, adding water or beef broth if the mixture appears too dry. Adjust the seasoning with salt and cayenne.

Serve the chili hot in bowls sprinkled with cheese and crushed corn chips. Pass the Tabasco at the table.

Chicken Comes Home to Roost

BY WILLIAM THOMAS COMPTON

It is both surprising and unsettling that Sookie Stackhouse, a human—albeit a very special human—can make me nervous. So I planned everything to a tee. I made reservations at the finest restaurant in Renard Parish, Maison de Paris. I chose the table with the best view of their famed marshland flora. I picked the entrée, coq au vin. And because I wanted nobody else to share in our time together, I paid the owner to have the restaurant all to ourselves for the entire night. Assuming that the experiences of the past few weeks haven't scared Sookie away from supernatural beings, I'm hoping that she'll join me in Vermont to take my hand in marriage.

MAKES 4 TO 6 SERVINGS

Marinade

ONE 750-ML BOTTLE	PINOT NOIR
2 CUPS	THINLY SLICED YELLOW ONION
1 CUP	COARSELY CHOPPED CELERY
1 CUP	COARSELY CHOPPED CARROT
2	GARLIC CLOVES, PEELED AND CRUSHED
1 TEASPOON	BLACK PEPPERCORNS

Chicken

5½ TO 6 POUNDS	CUT-UP CHICKEN OR A MIX OF BONE-IN CHICKEN BREASTS AND THIGHS
2 TABLESPOONS	OLIVE OIL
6 OUNCES	SLAB BACON, CUT INTO SMALL DICE
3 TABLESPOONS	ALL-PURPOSE FLOUR
3 TABLESPOONS	MINCED SHALLOT
1 TABLESPOON	MINCED GARLIC
3	FRESH THYME SPRIGS
3	FRESH FLAT-LEAF PARSLEY SPRIGS
4	BAY LEAVES
2 CUPS	CHICKEN BROTH
4 TABLESPOONS	UNSALTED BUTTER
1 POUND	WHITE BUTTON MUSHROOMS, WIPED CLEAN AND STEMMED
1 POUND	BOILING ONIONS, PEELED
SALT	
FRESHLY GROUND BLACK PEPPER	

2 TABLESPOONS	CHOPPED FRESH FLAT-LEAF PARSLEY

Make the marinade: Combine the ingredients in a large pot. Bring to boil over high heat. Reduce the heat to medium and simmer for 5 minutes. Remove from the heat and cool completely.

Make the chicken: Put the chicken pieces in a large nonreactive bowl and pour in the marinade. Turn to coat the chicken evenly. Cover and refrigerate at least 24 hours, turning the chicken occasionally in the marinade.

Transfer the chicken pieces to paper towels to drain, and pat with paper towels to dry. Strain the marinade, reserving the vegetables and marinade separately.

Heat the olive oil over medium-high heat in a pot large enough to accommodate the chicken in a single layer. Add the bacon and cook until crisp, about 3 minutes. Transfer the bacon to paper towels to drain. In batches, put the chicken skin-side down in the bacon drippings and brown evenly, about 8 minutes per side. Transfer the browned chicken to a large bowl.

Add the vegetables reserved from the marinade to the pot, and cook over medium-high heat, stirring, until soft and brown, about 10 minutes. Add the flour and cook, stirring, for 2 minutes. Gradually whisk in the reserved marinade liquid and bring to a boil, stirring constantly. Cook, still stirring, until the sauce thickens, about 2 minutes.

Add the shallot, garlic, thyme, parsley, and bay leaves. Stir to mix, and add the broth. Return the chicken to the pot, skin-side up, in a single layer. Bring the broth to a gentle simmer and reduce the heat to medium-low. Cover the pot and simmer for 30 minutes. Turn the chicken over, cover, and simmer until very tender, 15 to 20 minutes more.

Meanwhile, melt 3 tablespoons of the butter in a large, heavy skillet over medium heat. Add the mushrooms and cook, stirring, until tender, about 3 minutes. Transfer the mushrooms to a platter. Melt the remaining 1 tablespoon butter in the same skillet and add the onions. Cook, stirring, until the onions begin to brown and caramelize, 6 to 8 minutes. Transfer the onions to the platter with the mushrooms.

Transfer the chicken to another platter. Strain the sauce from the pot into the skillet, pressing on the solids to extract all the juices. Discard the solids. Bring the sauce to a simmer, scraping up the browned bits on the bottom of the skillet. Return the sauce to the pot, and add the mushrooms, onions, and bacon. Simmer, uncovered, until the sauce thickens slightly, 8 to 10 minutes.

Skim off any fat that has risen to the surface. Return the chicken to the pot and season with salt and pepper. Simmer for a few minutes to warm the chicken.

Arrange the chicken on a large serving platter and spoon the sauce and vegetables over. Garnish with the parsley and serve.

EVERYONE LOVES PIE

BY SOOKIE STACKHOUSE

Eventually you gotta take matters into your own hands. Sam offered to protect me, and that was sweet 'n' all, but he couldn't look out for me twenty-four hours a day, seven days a week. So I made up my mind to find the killer who took my friend Dawn and my brother's girlfriend Amy. I wasn't going to wait around to get strangled, stabbed, shot, or worse. Funny that the one clue that I got was when the killer attacked me. I saw in his mind an image of a woman. Her name was Cindy and she worked at Big Patty's Pie House. She seemed so sad and surprised when he killed her, like she knew him. Me and Sam drove down to Big Patty's, right off I-49, just south of Bon Temps. They had pies I'd never heard of: Frozen Hawaii Pie, Spunky Hollow Honey Pineapple Pie, Texas Special Sawdust Pie, Seven-Layer Jell-O Pie, and a bunch of other familiar ones like Chess Pie and Fresh Strawberry Pie. Turns out one of the customers knew Cindy. Told us she'd been murdered two years ago, just a little while after she and her brother moved to the area. Seems he didn't like her carrying on with vampires. That customer didn't seem to think too kindly of poor Cindy, but I kept my mouth shut long enough to get the killer's name: Drew Marshall. I made Sam promise me that once the case was solved and things calmed down, we'd come back so I could get a piece of that yummy-looking Jell-O pie.

Fried Apple Pies

Pastry

3 CUPS	ALL-PURPOSE FLOUR
1½ TEASPOONS	SALT
¾ TEASPOON	BAKING POWDER
6 TABLESPOONS	VEGETABLE SHORTENING, IN 6 PIECES, CHILLED
1	LARGE EGG
¾ CUP	WHOLE MILK

Filling

2 TABLESPOONS	UNSALTED BUTTER
2 TABLESPOONS	PACKED LIGHT BROWN SUGAR
2 TABLESPOONS	BRANDY, RUM, OR BOURBON
2	GRANNY SMITH APPLES, PEELED, CORED, AND DICED (ABOUT 2 CUPS)
1 TEASPOON	FRESH LEMON JUICE
1 TEASPOON	GROUND CINNAMON

8 CUPS	VEGETABLE OIL
2 TABLESPOONS	GRANULATED SUGAR
1 TEASPOON	GROUND CINNAMON

Make the pastry: Sift the flour, salt, and baking powder into a mixing bowl. Using a pastry blender, cut in the shortening until the mixture resembles coarse meal. In a small bowl, beat the egg with the milk. Gradually add the egg mixture to the flour mixture, stirring with a fork to make a thick dough. Form the dough into a disk, wrap in plastic wrap, and refrigerate for at least 2 hours.

Divide the dough into four equal portions. On a lightly floured work surface, roll out each portion into a round, about ⅛ inch thick. Using a saucer or small plate as a guide, cut out four 5-inch rounds. Dust off any excess flour with a pastry brush. Put the rounds on a parchment paper–lined baking sheet or large platter and refrigerate for at least 15 minutes. Gather the dough scraps and repeat the process, cutting out four more 5-inch rounds. Add the rounds to the baking sheet or platter in the refrigerator.

Make the filling: Melt the butter in a medium saucepan over medium heat. Add the brown sugar and stir until the mixture thickens slightly, about 2 minutes. Add the brandy and cook, stirring, for about 30 seconds. Add the apples and cook, stirring, for a couple of minutes until they begin to soften. Add the lemon juice and cinnamon and cook, stirring, until the apples are soft and caramelized, 4 to 6 minutes. Remove from the heat and let cool to room temperature.

Put 2 tablespoons of the apple mixture in the center of each round of dough. Lightly moisten the edges with cool water and fold the dough over the filling to form a half circle. Press the edges to seal, and crimp with your fingers or with the tines of a fork.

Heat the vegetable oil in a large, heavy pot or electric fryer until it registers 360°F on a deep-fry thermometer. In a small bowl, combine the sugar and cinnamon. Fry the pies two at a time, turning occasionally, until golden brown, about 5 minutes. Drain on paper towels and sprinkle with cinnamon-sugar. Serve warm.

Classic Chess Pie

3 CUPS	....	SUGAR
½ CUP (1 STICK)	....	UNSALTED BUTTER, AT ROOM TEMPERATURE
5	....	LARGE EGGS, LIGHTLY BEATEN
3 TABLESPOONS	....	YELLOW CORNMEAL
2 TEASPOONS	....	VANILLA EXTRACT
⅛ TEASPOON	....	SALT
1 CUP	....	WHOLE MILK
1	....	9-INCH UNBAKED PIE SHELL, HOMEMADE OR STORE-BOUGHT (THAWED IF FROZEN)

Preheat the oven to 325°F.

Combine the sugar and butter in a large mixing bowl, and beat on low speed with an electric mixer until well blended. Beat in the eggs, cornmeal, vanilla, and salt. Add the milk and beat on low speed until blended. Pour the mixture into the pie shell.

Bake until the filling is set when the pie is gently jiggled and a toothpick inserted into the center comes out clean, about 1¼ hours. (While the pie is baking, cover the edge with aluminum foil if the crust is browning too quickly.)

Let cool to room temperature, slice into wedges, and serve.

Glazed Fresh Strawberry Pie

Pastry

1 ⅓ CUPS	....	ALL-PURPOSE FLOUR
½ TEASPOON	....	SALT
½ CUP	....	VEGETABLE SHORTENING
3 TABLESPOONS	....	ICE WATER

*MAKES ONE 9-INCH PIE,
6 SERVINGS*

Filling and Glaze

3 ½ CUPS	....	HALVED FRESH STRAWBERRIES (ABOUT 1 QUART WHOLE STRAWBERRIES)
½ CUP	....	SUGAR
2 TABLESPOONS	....	CORNSTARCH
⅛ TEASPOON	....	SALT
¼ CUP PLUS 2 TABLESPOONS	....	WATER
6 OUNCES	....	CREAM CHEESE, AT ROOM TEMPERATURE
2 TABLESPOONS	....	FRESH ORANGE JUICE

SWEETENED WHIPPED CREAM FOR GARNISH (OPTIONAL)

Make the pastry: Combine the flour and salt in a medium mixing bowl. Cut in the shortening with a pastry blender or two knives until the mixture resembles coarse meal. Sprinkle with the water, 1 tablespoon at a time. Toss lightly with a fork until you can gather the dough into a ball. Flatten the dough to form a 6-inch disk, wrap in plastic wrap, and refrigerate for 30 minutes.

Preheat the oven to 425°F. Lightly flour a work surface and a rolling pin. Roll out the dough into a circle about 11 inches in diameter. Place the pie plate upside down in the center of the dough and trim the dough so that it is 1 inch larger than the pie plate. Fold the dough into quarters and transfer to the pie plate. Unfold the dough and press into the pie plate. Fold the edges under and flute them with your fingers.

Prick the bottom and sides of the dough randomly with a fork to prevent shrinkage. Bake until lightly browned, 10 to 15 minutes. Remove from the oven and let cool completely.

Make the filling and glaze: Set aside 2 cups of the strawberry halves. In a medium bowl, crush the remaining 1 ½ cups with a fork. In a small saucepan, combine the sugar, cornstarch, and salt. Gradually add the water, stirring until smooth. Add the crushed strawberries. Bring to a gentle boil over medium heat, stirring. Cook, continuing to stir, for 1 minute. Pour the mixture through a fine-mesh strainer into a bowl, pressing on the berries to extract as much liquid as possible. Set the bowl in a larger bowl containing ice water until the glaze is cool.

In a medium mixing bowl, beat the cream cheese with an electric mixer at medium speed until fluffy. Gradually add the orange juice and beat until smooth. Spread the mixture in the bottom of the baked piecrust. Arrange the reserved strawberry halves over the cream cheese filling and pour the cooked strawberry glaze over the strawberry halves. Refrigerate for at least 3 hours before serving.

Garnish each serving with a spoonful of whipped cream if you wish.

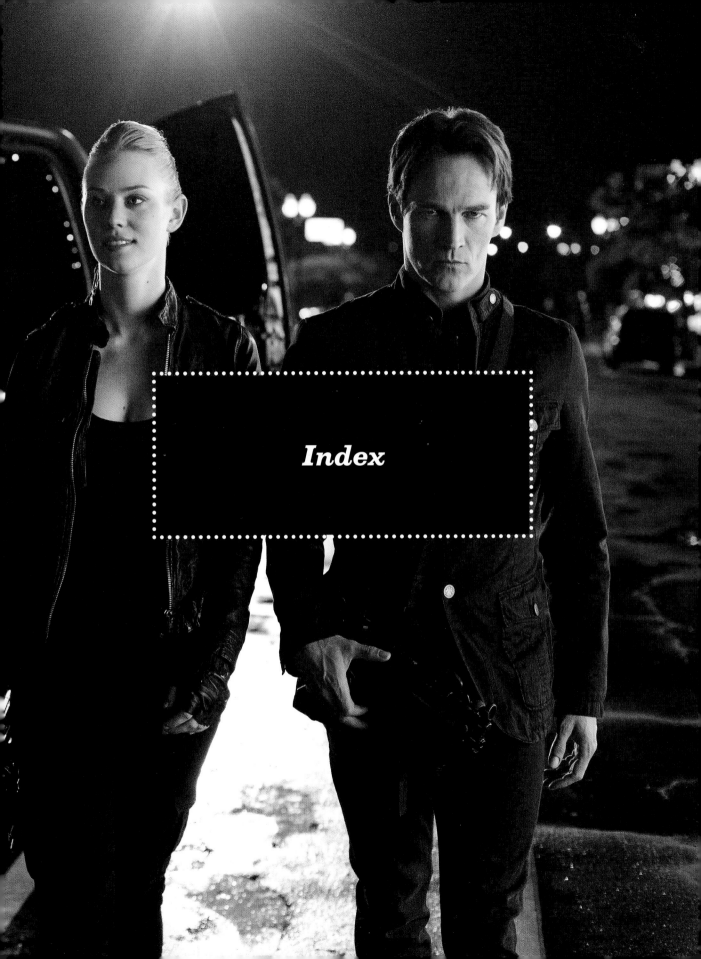

Index

Table of Equivalents

The exact equivalents in the following tables have been rounded for convenience.

LIQUID/DRY MEASUREMENTS

U.S.	Metric
¼ teaspoon	1.25 milliliters
½ teaspoon	2.5 milliliters
1 teaspoon	5 milliliters
1 tablespoon (3 teaspoons)	15 milliliters
1 fluid ounce (2 tablespoons)	30 milliliters
¼ cup	60 milliliters
⅓ cup	80 milliliters
½ cup	120 milliliters
1 cup	240 milliliters
1 pint (2 cups)	480 milliliters
1 quart (4 cups, 32 ounces)	960 milliliters
1 gallon (4 quarts)	3.84 liters
1 ounce (by weight)	28 grams
1 pound	448 grams
2.2 pounds	1 kilogram

LENGTHS

U.S.	Metric
⅛ inch	3 millimeters
¼ inch	6 millimeters
½ inch	12 millimeters
1 inch	2.5 centimeters

OVEN TEMPERATURE

Fahrenheit	Celsius	Gas
250	120	½
275	140	1
300	150	2
325	160	3
350	180	4
375	190	5
400	200	6
425	220	7
450	230	8
475	240	9
500	260	10

About the Creative Team

Alan Ball *is the creator, writer, and producer of the HBO original series* True Blood. *Ball also created, wrote, and produced the HBO series* Six Feet Under, *and wrote the screenplays for the Academy Award–winning film* American Beauty *and critically acclaimed independent film* Towelhead, *which he also directed. His work has received widespread praise, earning him an Academy Award, as well as multiple Emmys and Golden Globes. Though he now lives and works in Los Angeles, he has deep Southern roots, having grown up eating good Southern food in Marietta, Georgia.*

Gianna Sobol *is an associate producer on HBO's hit show* True Blood. *She writes for* HBO.com *and edits the* New York Times–*bestselling* True Blood *graphic novels.*

Benjamin Hayes *is the writers' assistant for HBO's* True Blood *and an independent screenwriter.*

Karen Sommer Shalett *is the editor in chief of* DC *magazine. The former Louisiana resident was a lifestyle editor at New Orleans'* Times-Picayune.

Marcelle Bienvenu *is a Louisiana native and cooking school teacher, who has written and tested recipes for many cookbooks, including the bestselling New Orleans heritage cookbook* Cookin' Up a Storm, *published by Chronicle Books.*

Alex Farnum *is a food and lifestyle photographer based on the West Coast.*